제2판

액션시리즈로 배우는

생활영어

김성애 지음

KM 경문사

서문

국제화, 세계화 물결 속에서 오늘을 살고 있는 현대인들에게는 각자의 분야에서 원활한 역할 수행을 위해 국제어인 영어로 의사소통할 줄 아는 능력이 필수적입니다. 하지만 일상생활 속에서 언어를 사용하면서 배울 수 있는 자연스런 언어 환경과는 달리, 우리나라에서는 실제 생활 속에서 의사소통의 수단으로 영어를 사용하는 환경이 아니기 때문에 이러한 능력을 기르는 일이 결코 쉬운 일은 아닙니다.

언어를 습득하는 데 가장 필요한 기본 요건은 상황 속에서의 충분한 언어 입력입니다. 다시 말하자면 말을 할 수 있기 위해서는 충분히 들을 기회를 가져야 합니다. 이런 점에서 본다면 일상생활 속에서 영어를 사용할 기회 자체가 거의 없는 우리나라와 같은 언어 환경에서, 더구나 문법을 위주로 공부한 사람들은 말할 기회가 와도 말이 쉽게 나오지 않는 것이 당연한 결과일 것입니다.

이 책은 영어 구사력을 높이고자 하는 학습자 여러분이 평소 생활 속에서 듣지 못하는 생활영어 표현을 스스로에게 제공하여 여러분이 처한 제한된 언어 환경을 다소나마 스스로 극복할 수 있도록 돕기 위한 것입니다. 이를 위하여 평소 생활 속에서 경험할 수 있는 여러 가지 상황을 중심으로 생활영어 표현들을 수록하였습니다. 결코 충분하다고는 할 수 없지만 아무쪼록 이 책에 실린 영어 표현들이 여러분의 영어 구사력을 높이는 데 다소나마 도움이 될 수 있기를 기원합니다.

저자 씀

저자가 추천하는 **이 책의 사용방법**

이 책에는 총 100개의 액션시리즈가 포함되어 있으며 각 액션시리즈는 두 페이지로 구성되어 있다. 앞 페이지에는 학습자가 상황을 이해하는 데 도움이 될 그림과 함께 최종적으로 익혀야 할 영어 표현들이 담긴 액션시리즈가 있다. 뒤 페이지에는 학습자가 액션시리즈를 익히기 위해 필요한 연습에 도움을 주기 위하여 괄호가 포함된 액션시리즈와 한글 번역이 있다. 구체적으로 저자가 추천하는 이 책의 사용 방법은 다음과 같다.

제1단계. 각 액션시리즈의 앞 페이지에 있는 영어로 된 액션시리즈를 보기 전에 뒤 페이지에 있는 한글 번역 부분을 보고 스스로 영어 표현을 만들어 본다. 이때 한글 번역에 너무 얽매이지 않는 것이 좋다. 왜냐하면 영어식 표현과 한국어식 표현이 다른 경우가 많아서 그대로 옮기다가는 어색한 표현이 될 수 있기 때문이다.

제2단계. 위의 제1단계에서 스스로의 힘으로는 영어 표현이 잘 안 되는 경우가 많을 것이다. 이때 앞 페이지에 있는 영어 표현을 보면서 자신이 몰랐던 부분이 어떤 것이었는지, 내가 만든 표현과 어떤 차이가 있는지 확인하면서 영어 표현을 익힌다. 아래에 제시되어 있는 어휘나 표현들의 도움을 받으며, 거의 외울 수 있을 정도로 여러 번 반복해서 연습하는 것이 좋다. 이때 액션시리즈가 묘사하는 상황을 머릿속으로 그려가며 표현을 익히는 것이 기억에 도움이 될 것이다.

제3단계. 어느 정도 표현에 자신이 생기면 다시 뒤 페이지로 넘어가서 아래 해석을 참고로 하면서 빈칸을 스스로의 힘으로 채워본다. 이때 잘 안 되면 앞 페이지로 돌아가서 다시 반복해서 익힌다.

제4단계. 뒤 페이지의 아래쪽 한글 번역 부분만 보면서 영어로 표현을 할 수 있는지 확인한다. 이는 한 번만으로 그칠 것이 아니라, 책을 늘 가까이에 두고 시간 날 때마다 반복해서 표현을 완전히 자기 것으로 만드는 것이 필요하다.

제5단계. 이 책의 궁극적인 목적은 학습자 여러분이 이 책을 보지 않고도 생활 속에서 유사한 상황에 처했을 때 영어로 표현하는 능력을 갖게 하는 것이다. 따라서 학습자 여러분은 이 책에서 배운 표현을 가능한 자주 생활 속의 상황과 연결하여 영어로 생각하고 표현하는 습관을 기르는 것이 좋다. 더불어 책에 소개된 상황뿐만 아니라 여러분이 경험하게 되는 새로운 상황도 나름대로 영어로 표현하려는 노력이 늘 필요하다.

이 책에서 강조하는 바는 영어를 사용할 수 있기 위해서는 우선 필요한 표현을 알고 있어야 한다는 것이다. 알지 못하는 표현을 사용할 수는 없다. 따라서 다양한 영어 표현을 아는 것이 중요하며, 그 표현들을 암기할 수 있을 정도로 반복 연습하라는 것이 이 책의 요지이다. 혹자는 암기에 대해 부정적으로 말하는 경우가 있으나 이는 아마도 기계적인 암기를 두고 하는 말일 것이다. 암기는 그 자체가 목적이 되어서는 안 되며, 연습의 결과가 되어야 한다. 기계적인 암기가 아니라 상황과 내용을 이해하면서 반복 연습하는 것은 매우 필요하다. 왜냐하면 우리나라와 같이 외국어로서 영어를 학습해야 하는 EFL(English as a Foreign Language) 환경에서는 제공받기 힘든, 하지만 언어습득을 위해서 없어서는 안 될 언어입력을 학습자 스스로 제공하는 효과가 있기 때문이다. 결국 우리나라와 같은 언어 환경에서 영어를 잘하는 비결은 시간과 노력을 투자하는 길밖에 없다고 생각한다. 다만 그 시간과 노력이 필요한 부분에 투자되어야 한다는 점이 중요하다. 그런 점에서 이 책이 영어를 배우고자 애쓰는 학습자들에게 조금이나마 도움이 되기를 바라는 마음이다.

차례

SECTION 1 At Home

SECTION 2 At Work

SECTION 3 Health&Leisure

SECTION 5 Shopping&Money

SECTION 6 Travel&Transportation

SECTION 7 Communication&Socializing

APPENDICES

SECTION 1

At Home

01 Brushing Your Teeth

A

1. Go into the bathroom.
2. Pick up your toothbrush.
3. Turn on the water.
4. Run some water over your toothbrush.
5. Turn off the water.
6. Squeeze some toothpaste on your toothbrush.
7. Brush your teeth with the toothbrush.
8. Move your toothbrush up and down.
9. Move your toothbrush back and forth.
10. Turn on the water again and rinse your mouth.
11. Rinse off your toothbrush.
12. Turn off the water.
13. Put your toothbrush back.

Key Vocabulary

- go into ~: ~로 들어가다
- pick up ~: ~을 집어 들다
- turn on/off ~: ~을 틀다, 켜다/잠그다, 끄다
- run some water over ~: ~위로 물을 흘려보내다
- rinse off ~: (비누, 불순물 등을) ~에서 씻어내다
- move : 움직이다, 옮기다
- up and down: 아래위로
- back and forth: 앞뒤로
- put ~ back: ~을 제자리에 놓다

B

1. Go _______ the bathroom.
2. _________ up your toothbrush.
3. _________ on the water.
4. _________ some water over your toothbrush.
5. Turn ______ the water.
6. _____________ some toothpaste on your toothbrush.
7. __________ your teeth with the toothbrush.
8. Move your toothbrush ________ and _________.
9. Move your toothbrush ________ and _________.
10. __________ on the water again and rinse your mouth.
11. Rinse ______ your toothbrush.
12. Turn _______ the water.
13. Put your toothbrush __________.

C

1. 욕실로 들어가세요.
2. 칫솔을 집으세요.
3. 물을 트세요.
4. 칫솔에 물을 좀 묻히세요.
5. 물을 잠그세요.
6. 칫솔에 치약을 좀 짜세요.
7. 칫솔로 이를 닦으세요.
8. 칫솔을 아래위로 움직이세요.
9. 칫솔을 앞뒤로 움직이세요.
10. 물을 다시 틀고 입을 헹구세요.
11. 칫솔을 헹구세요.
12. 물을 잠그세요.
13. 칫솔을 제자리에 놓으세요.

02 Going to Bed

A

1. It is late at night.
2. It was a long day today and you are tired now.
3. Yawn.
4. Say "Good night." to your family.
5. Go to your room and change into your nightgown.
6. Turn on the bedside lamp.
7. Turn off the room light.
8. Get into bed.
9. Set the alarm clock for 6 o'clock.
10. Put it on the nightstand.
11. Turn off the bedside lamp.
12. Lie down and fall asleep.

Key Vocabulary

- a long day: 긴 하루, 피곤한 날
- tired: 피곤한
- change into ~ : ~로 갈아입다
- nightgown: 잠옷
- room light: 방의 전등
- get into ~: ~ 속으로 들어가다
- bedside lamp: 침대 옆 램프
- turn on/off: 켜다/끄다
- set the alarm clock for ~ : 자명종을 ~시에 맞추다
- put A on B: A를 B위에 놓다
- lie down: 눕다
- fall asleep: 잠들다

B

1. It is late at night.
2. It was a ________ day today and you are tired now.
3. ___________.
4. Say "Good night." to your family.
5. Go to your room and ___________ into your nightgown.
6. Turn ______ the bedside lamp.
7. Turn ______ the room light.
8. Get ________ bed.
9. ________ the alarm clock for 6 o'clock.
10. Put it on the nightstand.
11. _________ off the bedside lamp.
12. _________ down and _________ asleep.

C

1. 밤이 늦었습니다.
2. 오늘 하루는 힘들었고 당신은 지금 피곤합니다.
3. 하품을 하세요.
4. 부모님께 “안녕히 주무세요.”라고 인사하세요.
5. 방으로 가서 잠옷으로 갈아입으세요.
6. 침대 옆 램프를 켜세요.
7. 방 전등은 끄세요.
8. 침대 속으로 들어가세요.
9. 알람시계를 6시로 맞추세요.
10. 침대 옆 탁자에 그것을 올려놓으세요.
11. 침대 옆 램프를 끄세요.
12. 누워서 잠드세요.

03 Taking a Shower

A

1. Go into the shower and pull the shower curtain shut.
2. Turn on the warm water.
3. Wash your hair with shampoo.
4. Wash the rest of your body with soap.
5. Rinse off with water.
6. Turn the water off and step out of the shower.
7. Take a towel from the towel rack.
8. Dry yourself off.
9. Wrap a towel around yourself.
10. Dry your hair with a blow-dryer.
11. Put on some body lotion.

Key Vocabulary

- shower: 샤워, 샤워장
- pull ~ shut: ~을 당겨서 닫다
- turn on/off ~: ~을 틀다, 켜다/잠그다, 끄다
- the rest of ~: ~의 나머지 부분
- rinse off with~: ~로 헹구다
- step out of ~: ~에서 나오다, 발을 빼다
- take A from B: B에서 A를 잡다, 가져오다
- tower rack: 수건 걸대
- dry ~ off: ~에서 물기를 제거하다, 말리다, 건조시키다
- wrap A around B: B둘레를 A로 감싸다
- put on~: ~을 바르다, 입다, 쓰다, 신다, 등등

B

1. Go into the __________ and _______ the shower curtain shut.
2. ____________ _________ the warm water.
3. Wash your hair _________ shampoo.
4. Wash the _________ of your body with soap.
5. Rinse ________ with water.
6. ________ the water off and step ______ ________ the shower.
7. ___________ a towel from the towel ________.
8. Dry yourself ________.
9. Wrap a towel __________ yourself.
10. _________ your hair with a blow-dryer.
11. ________ on some body lotion.

C

1. 샤워실로 들어가서 샤워 커튼을 당겨서 닫으세요.
2. 따뜻한 물을 트세요.
3. 샴푸로 머리를 감으세요.
4. 몸의 나머지 부분을 비누로 씻으세요.
5. 물로 헹구세요.
6. 물을 끄고 샤워장에서 나오세요.
7. 수건 걸대에서 수건을 집으세요.
8. 몸의 물기를 닦으세요.
9. 수건으로 몸을 감싸세요.
10. 드라이기로 머리를 말리세요.
11. 몸에 바디로션을 좀 바르세요.

04 Cleaning the House

A

1. Boy, your house sure is dirty!
2. Put on your apron.
3. Sprinkle some kitchen cleanser in the sink.
4. Scrub the sink with a sponge.
5. Sweep the kitchen floor with a broom.
6. Mop the kitchen floor.
7. Dust the furniture with a dust cloth.
8. Empty the wastebaskets.
9. Plug in the vacuum cleaner.
10. Turn it on.
11. Vacuum the rugs and carpets.
12. Put all the cleaning stuff away.
13. Look around. It looks much better now!

Key Vocabulary

- Boy!: 아이고! 어머나! 저런!
- sure: 정말로
- sprinkle: 흩뿌리다
- put on the apron: 앞치마를 착용하다
- kitchen cleanser: 부엌 세척제
- scrub A with B: B로 A를 문지르다
- fill A with B: B로 A를 채우다
- empty: 비우다
- plug in ~: ~의 전기 플러그를 꽂다
- put away ~: ~을 치우다
- cleaning stuff: 청소에 사용된 물건들, 청소용품
- look around~: ~을 둘러보다
- look better: 더 좋아 보인다
- much better: 훨씬 더 좋은

B

1. Boy, your house __________ is dirty!
2. _________ on your apron.
3. ______________ some kitchen cleanser in the sink.
4. ____________ the sink with a sponge.
5. ____________ the kitchen floor with a broom.

6. _________ the kitchen floor.
7. ___________ the furniture with a dust cloth.
8. ____________ the wastebaskets.
9. __________ ________ the vacuum cleaner.

10. Turn it _____.
11. ______________ the rugs and carpets.
12. ________ all the cleaning stuff away.

13. Look ___________. It looks much better!

C

1. 아이고! 집이 정말 더럽네요.
2. 앞치마를 착용하세요.
3. 싱크대에 부엌 세척제를 좀 뿌리세요.
4. 스펀지로 싱크대를 문지르세요.
5. 빗자루로 부엌 바닥을 쓰세요.
6. 부엌 바닥을 밀대 걸레로 미세요.
7. 걸레로 가구의 먼지를 닦아내세요.
8. 쓰레기통을 비우세요.
9. 진공청소기를 전원에 꽂으세요.
10. 켜세요.
11. 양탄자와 카페트를 진공청소하세요.
12. 모든 청소용품을 치우세요.
13. 둘러보세요. 훨씬 좋아 보입니다!

05 Changing the Light bulb

A

1. You have tons of work to do.
2. Sit at the desk and turn on the light.

3. It doesn't work. What's wrong?
4. Check the lamp. Oh, it's burned out!
5. You need to change the light bulb.
6. Go get a new one.
7. Unplug the lamp and take off the lamp shade.
8. Unscrew the old bulb.
9. Screw the new one into the socket.

10. Put the lamp shade back on.
11. Plug in the lamp and turn it on.

12. It works!
13. Throw the old bulb away and get to work.

Key Vocabulary

- tons of ~: 많은 ~
- work: 작동하다
- What's wrong?: 무엇이 잘못되었지?
- burn out: 타다
- It's(=It has) burned out: 타버렸다.
- go get ~: 가서 ~을 가져오다
- unplug: 플러그를 뽑다
- take off ~: ~을 벗기다
- unscrew: 돌려서 빼다
- screw A into B: A를 B 속에 돌려서 끼워넣다
- put ~ on: ~을 씌우다, 입히다
- put ~ back on: 도로 씌우다
- plug in: 플러그를 끼우다
- It works: 작동한다.
- throw ~ away: ~을 버리다
- get to work: 일을 시작하다

B

1. You have ________ of work to do.
2. Sit at the desk and ________ ______ the light.
3. It doesn't ________. What's _________?
4. Check the lamp. Oh, it's ___________ out!
5. You need to __________ the light bulb.
6. Go _________ a new one.
7. __________ the lamp and take off the lamp _________.
8. _____________ the old bulb.
9. Screw the new one ___________ the socket.
10. Put the lamp shade __________ on.
11. __________ in the lamp and turn it _____.
12. It __________!
13. Throw the old bulb __________ and get ______ work.

C

1. 당신은 할 일이 무척 많습니다.
2. 책상에 앉아서 전등을 켜세요.
3. 불이 안 나옵니다. 무엇이 잘못되었지?
4. 전등을 살펴보세요. 아, 타버렸네요!
5. 전구를 갈아야겠네요.
6. 가서 새것을 하나 가지고 오세요.
7. 전등 플러그를 빼고 전등갓을 벗기세요.
8. 낡은 전구는 돌려서 빼내세요.
9. 새 전구를 소켓 속으로 돌려 끼워 넣으세요.
10. 전등갓을 다시 씌우세요.
11. 전등 플러그를 꽂으세요.
12. 되네요!
13. 낡은 전구는 버리고, 일을 시작하세요.

06 Doing the Dishes

A

1. Stack up the dirty dishes.
2. Carry them to the kitchen.

3. Take the serving dishes off the table.
4. Put the leftovers into containers.
5. Put them into the refrigerator.
6. Scrape the scraps from the plates into the garbage.
7. Wipe the table off.
8. Put the plug into the drain in the sink.

9. Fill the sink with water.
10. Put some dish soap into the water.

11. Wash the dirty dishes.
12. Rinse the dishes.
13. Put the wet dishes in the rack and dry them.

Key Vocabulary

- stack up: 차곡차곡 쌓다
- take A off B: A를 B에서 치우다, 떼어내다
- put A into B: A를 B에 집어넣다
- scrape the scraps: 찌꺼기를 긁어내다
- wipe off: 닦다
- drain: 하수구
- put A into B: A를 B에 넣다, 끼우다
- fill A with B: A를 B로 채우다
- dish soap: 설거지용 세제
- dry: 건조시키다
- carry A to B: A를 B로 가져가다
- leftover: 남은 것
- plug: 플러그, 마개
- rack: 시렁, 선반

B

1. __________ up the dirty dishes.

2. __________ them to the kitchen.
3. Take the serving dishes _____ the table.
4. Put the ________________ into containers.
5. ________ them into the refrigerator.
6. __________ the scraps from the plates into the garbage.
7. Wipe the table ______.
8. Put the _________ into the drain in the sink.

9. ________ the sink with water.
10. Put some dish _______ into the water.

11. _________ the dirty dishes.
12. __________ the dishes.
13. Put the wet dishes in the dish __________.

C

1. 더러운 접시들을 쌓으세요.
2. 그것들을 부엌으로 운반하세요.
3. 서빙 접시들을 식탁에서 치우세요.
4. 남은 음식들을 용기에 담으세요.
5. 그것들을 냉장고에 넣으세요.
6. 접시에서 찌꺼기들을 긁어서 쓰레기에 버리세요.
7. 테이블을 닦으세요.
8. 싱크 안에 있는 하수구에 플러그를 끼우세요.
9. 싱크를 물로 채우세요.
10. 설거지용 세제를 물에 좀 넣으세요.
11. 더러운 접시를 씻으세요.
12. 접시들을 헹구세요.
13. 젖은 접시들을 접시 시렁(건조대)에 담으세요.

07 Doing Laundry

A

1. You need to do laundry.
2. Sort the laundry for dark colors and light colors.
3. Check the pockets of the pants and shirts and take out anything in them.
4. Put the laundry into the washing machine.
5. Adjust the settings on the machine.
6. Put in some detergent and turn on the machine.
7. The machine washes, rinses, and spins the laundry.
8. Now, time's up and the machine stops.
9. Take the wet clothes out of the machine.
10. Hang them out to dry.

Key Vocabulary

- do laundry: 세탁하다
- laundry: 세탁물
- sort A for B: A를 B로 구분하다
- take out: 끄집어내다
- put A into B: A를 B에 집어넣다
- adjust: 조절하다, 맞추다
- settings on the machine: 기계의 조절장치
- put in: 넣다
- detergent: 세제
- turn on: 켜다
- spin: 돌리다
- Time's(=Time is) up: 시간이 다 되다.
- take A out of B: A를 B에서 끄집어내다
- hang out: 밖에 널다
- dry: 마르다, 건조하다

B

1. You need to do ________________.
2. _________ the laundry for dark colors and light colors.
3. Check the pockets of the pants and shirts and _______ out nything in them.
4. ________ the laundry into the washing machine.
5. __________ the settings on the machine.
6. Put in some ____________ and ________ on the machine.
7. The machine washes, rinses, and spins the laundry.
8. Now, time's ______ and the machine stops.
9. Take the wet clothes _______ of the machine.
10. __________ them out to dry.

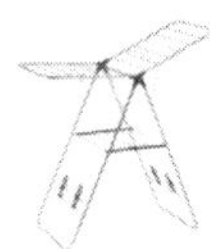

C

1. 당신은 세탁을 할 필요가 있네요.
2. 세탁물을 짙은 색과 옅은 색으로 구분하세요.
3. 바지와 셔츠의 주머니를 체크하고, 그 안에 있는 건 모두 끄집어내세요.
4. 세탁물을 세탁기에 집어넣으세요.
5. 기계의 세팅을 조절하세요.
6. 세제를 넣고 기계를 켜세요.
7. 기계가 세탁물을 씻고, 헹구고, 돌립니다.
8. 자, 시간이 다 되었고, 기계가 멈춥니다.
9. 젖은 세탁물을 기계에서 끄집어내세요.
10. 그것들을 밖에다 널어서 건조시키세요.

08 Leaving the House

A

1. You need to go out for an appointment.
2. Nobody else is at home.
3. Make sure all the windows are locked.
4. Check if you've turned off all the lights and the gas.
5. Turn the answering machine on.
6. Now, everything looks OK.
7. Pick up your bag and cell phone.
8. Put on your shoes.
9. Oops! You forgot your key. It's on the table.
10. Take off your shoes and pick it up.
11. Put on your shoes again.
12. Open the door, go out and close it.
13. Lock the door and leave.

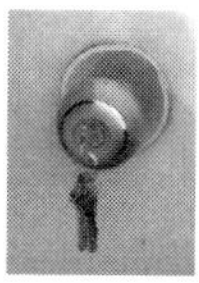

Key Vocabulary

- go out: 외출하다, 나가다
- appointment: (만남을 위한 시간적인) 약속
  (cf. promise: ~을 꼭 하겠다는 맹세, 약속)
- nobody else: 다른 누구도
- make sure ~: 꼭 ~하세요
- locked: 잠긴
- turn on/off: 켜다/끄다
- answering machine: 응답기
- pick up: 집어 들다
- forget: 깜박하다, 잊다
- cell phone; 휴대폰 (=mobile phone)
- Oops!: 어머나! 이런!
- put on: 신다
- take off: 벗다
- leave: 떠나다

B

1. You need to go out for an ________________.
2. Nobody ________ is at home.
3. Make _________ all the windows are locked.
4. Check if you've turned off all the lights and the gas.
5. Turn the answering machine _______.
6. Now, everything __________ OK.
7. _________ up your bag and cell phone.
8. Put _______ your shoes.
9. Oops! You ___________ your key.
   It's on the table.
10. _________ off your shoes and _______ it up.
11. _________ on your shoes, again.
12. Open the door, go out and close it.
13. __________ the door and leave.

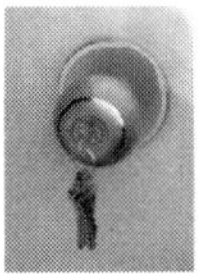

C

1. 당신은 약속이 있어서 외출해야 합니다.
2. 집에 아무도 없습니다.
3. 창문들이 모두 잠겼는지 확인하세요.
4. 전등과 가스가 모두 꺼졌는지 체크하세요.
5. 응답기를 트세요.
6. 이제 모든 게 좋아 보입니다.
7. 가방과 휴대폰을 챙기세요.
8. 신발을 신으세요.
9. 아차! 열쇠를 깜박했네요. 테이블 위에 있습니다.
10. 신발을 벗고 열쇠를 챙기세요.
11. 신발을 다시 신으세요.
12. 문을 열고 나가서 닫으세요.
13. 문을 잠그고 떠나세요.

09 The Alarm Clock

A

1. Your alarm clock didn't go off this morning.
2. What's wrong?
3. Pick up the clock and check it over.
4. Everything looks just fine but it doesn't work.
5. Oh! It must be the battery!
6. The battery was changed quite a long ago.
7. Go get a new battery.
8. Take off the battery cover.
9. Take out the old battery and put in the new one.
10. Check if the clock works.
11. Yes, it works!
12. Now, put the battery cover back on.
13. Throw the old one into the used battery box.

Key Vocabulary

- go off: 발사되다, 작동하다
- What's wrong?: 무엇이 잘못되었을까?
- check ~ over: ~을 살펴보다
- It look fine: 괜찮은 것 같다.
- work: 작동하다
- must be ~: ~임에 틀림없다
- quite a long ago: 꽤 오래 전에
- go get: 가지러 가다
- take off: 벗겨내다, 떼어내다
- take out: 끄집어내다
- put in: 집어넣다
- check if ~: ~인지 어떤지 점검하다
- put ~ back on: ~을 도로 씌우다
- throw A away into B: A를 B 속으로 버리다

B

1. Your alarm clock didn't go ______ this morning.
2. What's ____________?
3. _________ up the clock and check it _________.
4. Everything looks just fine but it doesn't _________.

5. Oh! It _________ be the battery!
6. The battery was changed quite a long ________.

7. Go _________ a new battery.
8. ___________ off the battery cover.
9. Take _______ the old battery and _____ in the new one.
10. Check ________ the clock works.
11. Yes, it ____________!
12. Now, put the battery cover _________ on.
13. ___________ the old one into the used battery box.

C

1. 오늘 아침 당신의 자명종이 울리지 않았어요.
2. 무엇이 잘못되었을까요?
3. 시계를 집어 들고 이리저리 살펴보세요.
4. 모두 괜찮은 것 같은데 시계가 안 가네요.
5. 아! 건전지 때문임에 틀림없어요!
6. 건전지를 꽤 오래 전에 교환했거든요.
7. 가서 새 건전지 하나를 가져 오세요.
8. 건전지 덮개를 떼세요.
9. 오래된 건전지를 빼내고 새것을 끼우세요.
10. 시계가 가는지 보세요.
11. 예! 가네요.
12. 이제 건전지 커버를 도로 씌우세요.
13. 오래된 건전지는 다 쓴 건전지 박스에 버리세요.

10 Returning to Home

A

1. Get back to your apartment building.
2. Check your mailbox and take out your mail.
3. Take the elevator up to your floor.
4. Get off the elevator.
5. Unlock the door with the apartment key.
6. Turn the doorknob and open the door.

7. Take off your shoes.
8. Put the bag down.
9. Take off your coat and hang it up.
10. Go to the living room.

11. Sit on the sofa.
12. Check for message on the answering machine.

Key Vocabulary

- get back to ~: ~로 돌아가다
- take out: 끄집어내다
- mail: 우편물
- take the elevator up to ~: ~까지 승강기를 타고가다
- get off ~ : ~에서 내리다
- unlock: (잠긴 것을 열쇠로) 열다
- doorknob: 문의 손잡이
- take off ~: ~을 벗다
- put down ~: 내려놓다
- hang up ~: ~을 걸다
- check for ~: ~에 대해 점검하다
- answering machine: 응답기

B

1. Get __________ to your apartment building.
2. Check your mailbox and take _________ your mail.
3. _____________ the elevator up to your floor.
4. _________ off the elevator.
5. ____________ the door with the apartment key.
6. Turn the __________ and open the door.

7. Take ________ your shoes.
8. Put the bag ___________.

9. _________ off your coat and hang it ______.
10. Go to the living room.
11. Sit on the sofa.
12. Check for message _____ the answering machine.

C

1. 아파트 건물로 돌아가세요.
2. 우편함을 점검하고 우편물을 끄집어내세요.
3. 엘리베이터를 타고 당신이 사는 층까지 올라가세요.
4. 엘리베이터에서 내리세요.
5. 아파트 열쇠로 문을 여세요.
6. 문 손잡이를 돌려서 문을 여세요.
7. 구두를 벗으세요.
8. 가방을 내려놓으세요.
9. 코트를 벗어서 거세요.
10. 거실로 가세요.
11. 소파에 앉으세요.
12. 응답기에 메시지가 있는지 점검하세요.

11 Taking Care of the Lawn

A

1. Fill the lawn mower's gas tank.
2. Pull the cord and start the mower.
3. Mow the lawn by pushing the mower back and forth.
4. The mower can't reach everywhere.
5. You have to use your own hand for some places.
6. Trim the grass by hand.
7. Rake up the grass clippings.
8. Put them on a compost pile.
9. A compost pile contains old leaves, grass, twigs, etc.
10. Spread some grass seeds on bare spots.
11. Water the lawn.
12. All done. It looks wonderful now!

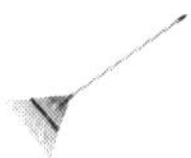

Key Vocabulary

- fill: 채우다
- mow the lawn: 잔디를 깎다
- reach: 닿다, 미치다
- rake up: 갈퀴로 긁어모으다
- clipping: 잘린/깎인 것
- compost pile: 퇴비 더미
- twig: 잔가지
- spread: 흩뿌리다
- seed: 씨앗
- bare spot: 비어있는 곳 (즉, 잔디가 없는 곳)
- water the lawn: 잔디에 물을 뿌리다
- pull: 당기다 (cf. push: 밀다)
- back and forth: 앞뒤로
- trim: 다듬다
- all done: 다 됐다.

B

1. _______ the lawn mower's gas tank.
2. ________ the cord and start the mower.
3. Mow the lawn by pushing the mower ______________.
4. The mower can't __________ everywhere.
5. Your have to use your own _______ for some places.
6. _________ the grass by hand.
7. __________ up the grass clippings.
8. Put them on a _________ pile.
9. A compost pile __________ old leaves, grass, twigs, etc.
10. _____________ some grass seeds on _________ spots.
11. ___________ the lawn.
12. All ________. It looks wonderful now!

C

1. 잔디 깎는 기계의 가스탱크를 채우세요.
2. 코드를 잡아당겨서 잔디 깎는 기계를 작동시키세요.
3. 잔디 깎는 기계를 앞뒤로 밀면서 잔디를 깎으세요.
4. 잔디 깎는 기계가 모든 곳에 다 닿을 수 있는 것은 아닙니다.
5. 몇 군데는 당신이 직접 자신의 손을 써야합니다.
6. 손으로 풀을 다듬으세요.
7. 풀에서 잘라낸 것들을 갈고리로 모으세요.
8. 그것들을 퇴비 더미에 쌓으세요.
9. 퇴비 더미는 낡은 잎, 풀, 잔나무가지 등을 포함하고 있습니다.
10. 땅이 드러난 부분에는 잔디 씨를 뿌리세요.
11. 잔디에 물을 주세요.
12. 다 됐습니다. 이제 정말 멋져 보입니다.

12 Checking the Mailbox

A

1. You are waiting for an important document.
2. It must arrive by today.
3. Check the mail box.

4. It's empty. The mail isn't in yet.
5. Wait for a while.

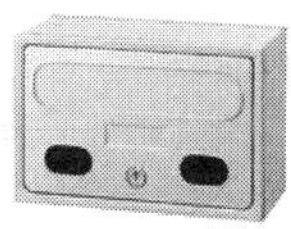

6. Check the mail box again.
7. Oh, something is in the box.
8. It must be the document.
9. Take out the mail and check if it is the document.
10. Oh, no! It is not what you want.
11. Do you think you must wait till tomorrow?
12. No! You'd better call and complain about it.

Key Vocabulary

- wait for ~: ~을 기다리다
- document: 서류
- by today: 오늘까지
- empty: 비어있는 (cf. full: 가득 찬)
- The mail is in: 우편물이 왔다.
- It must be ~: ~임에 틀림없다
- take out: 끄집어내다
- check if ~: ~인지 아닌지 점검하다
- what you want: 당신이 원하는 것
- till tomorrow: 내일까지
- You'd better ~: ~하는 게 낫다
- complain about~: ~에 대해 불평하다

B

1. You are waiting for an important ___________.
2. It must arrive _______ today.

3. Check the mail box.
4. It's __________. The mail isn't _____ yet.
5. Wait for a _________.

6. Check the mail box again.
7. Oh, something is in the box.
8. It _________ be the document.
9. Take ______ the mail and see ____ it is the document.
10. Oh, no! It is not what you want.
11. Do you think you must wait ________ tomorrow?
12. No! You'd _________ call and ___________ about it.

C

1. 당신은 중요한 서류를 기다리고 있습니다.
2. 오늘까지는 도착해야 합니다.
3. 우편함을 체크하세요.
4. 비었습니다. 우편이 아직 안 왔을 겁니다.
5. 조금만 기다리세요.
6. 다시 우편함을 체크하세요.
7. 아, 뭔가 들어있네요.
8. 그 서류임에 틀림없습니다.
9. 우편물을 끄집어내서 그 서류인지 체크하세요.
10. 이런! 당신이 원하는 것이 아니네요.
11. 다시 기다려야 하나요?
12. 아뇨! 전화 걸어서 불평하는 게 나아요.

13 A Broken Glass

A

1. You want to drink some juice in a new glass.
2. Try to take a new glass out of the cupboard.
3. Darn! You dropped the glass and broke it.

4. Pick up the big pieces first.
5. Be careful not to cut yourself!
6. Take them over to the garbage can and throw them away.
7. Bring the dustpan and the broom.

8. Sweep the small pieces into the dustpan.
9. Dump them into the garbage can.

10. Put the dustpan and the broom back.
11. Go get another glass.
12. Be careful! Don't drop it again!

Key Vocabulary

- take A out of B: A를 B에서 끄집어내다
- Darn!: 이런! 젠장! 빌어먹을!
- pick up: 줍다
- take A (over) to B: A를 B로 가져가다
- throw away: 버리다
- drop: 떨어뜨리다
- Be careful not to ~: ~하지 않도록 조심하다
- cut oneself: (칼로) 베다
- bring: 가져오다
- broom: 빗자루
- dustpan: 쓰레받기
- sweep A into B: A를 B에로 쓸어 담다
- dump A into B: A를 B 속으로 (던져)버리다
- put back: 제자리에 갖다 놓다
- go get: 가서 가져오다

B

1. You want to drink some juice in a new glass.
2. Try to take a new glass ______ of the cupboard.
3. Darn! You ___________ the glass and broke it.

4. Pick up the big _________ first.
5. Be careful not to _______ yourself!
6. _________ them over to the garbage can and _______ them away.
7. __________ the dustpan and the broom.

8. ___________ the small pieces into the dustpan.
9. Dump them ________ the garbage can.

10. Put the dustpan and the broom __________.
11. Go ________ another glass.
12. Be ___________! Don't drop it again!

C

1. 당신은 새 잔에다 쥬스를 마시고 싶습니다.
2. 찬장에서 새 잔을 하나 꺼내려 합니다.
3. 이런! 잔을 떨어뜨려서 잔이 깨집니다.
4. 큰 조각부터 먼저 주우세요.
5. 베이지 않도록 조심하세요.
6. 그것들을 쓰레기통으로 가져가서 버리세요.
7. 쓰레받기와 빗자루를 가져오세요.
8. 작은 조각들을 쓰레받기에 쓸어 담으세요.
9. 쓰레기통에 버리세요.
10. 쓰레받기와 빗자루를 제자리에 갖다놓으세요.
11. 가서 새 잔을 하나 가져오세요.
12. 조심하세요! 또 떨어뜨리지 마세요!

14 Getting Ready for Work

A

1. The alarm clock rings.
2. Wake up.
3. Stretch, yawn and rub your eyes.
4. Get off the bed and make the bed.
5. Go to the bathroom and wash your face.
6. Go back to your bedroom and put on some lotion.
7. Go to the kitchen and eat breakfast.
8. Go to the bathroom and brush your teeth.
9. Go back to your room and get dressed.
10. Pick up your bag, cell phone and car key.
11. Kiss your family goodbye.
12. Leave the house for work.

Key Vocabulary

- alarm clock: 자명종
- wake up: 잠이 깨다
- stretch: 기지개를 쭉 켜다
- yawn: 하품하다
- rub: 부비다
- get off: 내려오다
- make the bed: 침대를 정돈하다
- put on: 바르다
- get dressed: 옷을 입다
- pick up: 집어 들다
- cell phone: 휴대폰 (=mobile phone)
- kiss your family good bye: 가족에게 작별키스를 하다.
- leave A for B: B를 향하여 A를 떠나다

B

1. The ________ clock rings.

2. ________ up.
3. Stretch, yawn and _____ your eyes.
4. Get _______ the bed and _________ the bed.
5. Go to the bathroom and ________ your face.
6. Go back to your bedroom and _______ on some lotion.
7. Go to the kitchen and _______ breakfast.
8. Go to the bathroom and _________ your teeth.

9. Go back to your room and get ____________.

10. _______ up your bag, cell phone and car key.
11. Kiss your family ____________.
12. Leave the house _______ work.

C

1. 자명종이 울립니다.
2. 잠에서 깨세요.
3. 기지개를 켜고, 하품을 하고, 눈을 비비세요.
4. 침대에서 나와 침대를 정리하세요.
5. 욕실로 가서 세수를 하세요.
6. 방으로 돌아가서 로션을 좀 바르세요.
7. 부엌으로 가서 식사를 하세요.
8. 욕실로 가서 양치를 하세요.
9. 방으로 돌아가서 옷을 입으세요.
10. 가방과 휴대폰과 차 열쇠를 집어드세요.
11. 가족에게 작별 키스를 하세요.
12. 직장을 향해 집을 떠나세요.

15 A Power Failure

A

1. There's a severe thunderstorm at night.

2. The power went out and it's all dark.
3. Find a flashlight and turn it on.
4. Find some candles and light them.
5. Find the circuit-breaker box.
6. Open the box.
7. Check and find the breakers that had tripped.
8. Reset the breakers.

9. Good! The power came back on.
10. Close the circuit-breaker box.
11. Turn off the flashlight and extinguish the candles.
12. Put the flashlight and candles back to the place.

Key Vocabulary

- severe: 심한
- thunderstorm: (천둥번개를 동반한) 뇌우
- power: 전기
- go out: 나가다, 꺼지다
- It's all dark: 온통 어둡다.
- light: 불을 켜다, 불을 붙이다
- circuit-breaker box: 차단기 박스, 두꺼비집
- trip: 넘어지다
- reset: 제자리에 놓다
- come back on: 도로 오다
- turn off: (스위치로) 끄다
- extinguish: 불을 끄다
- put~ back to the place: ~을 제자리에 놓다

B

1. There's a severe ____________________ at night.
2. The power __________ _______ and it's all dark.
3. Find a flashlight and __________ it on.
4. Find some candles and ___________ them.
5. Find the _________________________ box.

6. Open the box.
7. Check and find the breakers that had _____________.
8. _____________ the breakers.
9. Good! The power came __________ on.

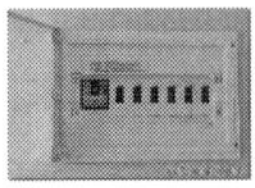

10. ___________ the circuit-breaker box.
11. Turn ______ the flashlight and ___________ the candles.
12. _______ the flashlight and candles back to the _______.

C

1. 밤에 심한 뇌우가 있습니다.
2. 전기가 나가고 온통 어둡습니다.
3. 손전등을 찾아서 켜세요.
4. 초들을 찾아서 불을 켜세요.
5. 차단기 박스를 찾으세요.
6. 박스 문을 여세요.
7. 살펴보고 내려진 브레이크들을 찾으세요.
8. 브레이크들을 제자리에 놓으세요.
9. 좋아요! 전기가 다시 들어왔습니다.
10. 차단기 박스를 닫으세요.
11. 손전등을 끄고 촛불도 끄세요.
12. 손전등과 초들을 제자리에 두세요.

SECTION 2

At Work

16 A Coffee Break

A

1. You are so tired and want to take a break.
2. Go get a cup of coffee.
3. Take your MP3 player and coffee to the lounge.
4. Have a seat away from other people.
5. Make yourself as comfortable as possible.
6. Put on the ear phone.
7. Choose an easy listening music.

8. Enjoy the music and coffee.
9. You finished your coffee but the break time is left.
10. Lean against the sofa and close your eyes.
11. Fall asleep right away.

12. Finally, somebody wakes you up.
13. "Oops! I didn't mean to sleep."
    Hurry to the office.

Key Vocabulary

- take a break: 휴식을 취하다
- go get ~: ~을 가지러 가다
- take A to B: A를 B로 가져가다
- have a seat: 앉다
- away from ~ : ~로부터 떨어져서
- as ~ as possible: 가능한 ~하게
- put on: 끼다, 착용하다
- easy listening music: 편안하게 들을 수 있는 음악
- lean against ~ : ~에 기대다
- fall asleep: 잠들다
- right away: 바로, 곧, 당장
- wake up: 깨다, 깨우다
- mean to ~: ~하려 하다
- hurry to ~: ~로 급히 가다

B

1. You are so tired and want to ________ a break.
2. Go ______ a cup of coffee.
3. ______ your MP3 player and coffee to the lounge.
4. Have a ________ away from other people.
5. Make yourself as comfortable as __________.

6. _______ on the ear phone.
7. Choose an ________ listening music.
8. Enjoy the music and coffee.
9. You _______ your coffee but the break time is ______.
10. Lean _________ the sofa and close your eyes.
11. _______ asleep right away.

12. Finally, somebody _________ you up.
13. "Oops! I didn't ________ to sleep."
    __________ to the office.

C

1. 당신은 너무 피곤해서 쉬고 싶습니다.
2. 가서 커피 한잔 가져오세요
3. MP3와 커피를 가지고 휴게실로 가세요.
4. 다른 사람들과 떨어져서 앉으세요.
5. 자신을 최대한 편하게 하세요.
6. 이어폰을 끼세요.
7. 편안한 음악을 고르세요.
8. 음악과 커피를 즐기세요.
9. 커피를 다 마셨지만 휴식시간이 남았네요.
10. 소파에 기대고 눈을 감으세요.
11. 바로 잠이 듭니다.
12. 마침내 누군가 당신을 깨웁니다.
13. "어머나! 잠을 자려고 했던 것이 아닌데."
    사무실로 급히 가세요.

17 At the Cafeteria

A

1. It's the lunch break.
2. Go to the cafeteria for lunch.
3. Oh, it's very crowded. Stand in line.
4. Finally, it's your turn.
5. Pick up a tray, a spoon and chopsticks.
6. Go to the food stand.
7. Pick up the rice, soup and side dishes.
8. Pick up a glass of water, too.
9. Look for an empty seat.
10. There's one! Go to the table.
11. Put down the tray on the table and sit down.
12. Take a sip of water and enjoy your lunch.

Key Vocabulary

- lunch break: 점심시간
- crowded: 복잡한, 붐비는
- your turn: 당신 차례
- chopsticks: 젓가락
- rice: 밥
- pick up: 집다
- empty: 비어있는
- a sip of water: 물 한 모금
- cafeteria: (학교, 회사 등의)식당
- stand in line: 줄을 서다
- tray: 쟁반
- food stand: 음식 진열대
- side dishes: 반찬들
- look for ~: ~을 찾다
- put down: 내려놓다

B

1. It's the lunch break.
2. Go to the cafeteria _______ lunch.
3. Oh, it's very _____________. Stand ______ line.
4. Finally, it's your _________.
5. Pick up a ________, a spoon and chopsticks.
6. Go to the food ____________.
7. Pick up the rice, soup and ________ dishes.
8. Pick up a glass _____ water, too.
9. Look ________ an empty seat.
10. There's ________! Go to the table.
11. Put ___________ the tray on the table and sit down.
12. ___________ a sip of water and enjoy your lunch.

C

1. 점심시간입니다.
2. 점심 먹으러 식당으로 가세요.
3. 아, 매우 복잡하네요. 줄을 서세요.
4. 마침내 당신 차례입니다.
5. 쟁반, 숟가락, 젓가락을 집으세요.
6. 음식 진열대로 가세요.
7. 밥, 국, 반찬들을 집으세요.
8. 물도 한 잔 집으세요.
9. 빈 좌석을 찾으세요.
10. 아, 저기 하나 있네요! 식탁으로 가세요.
11. 쟁반을 식탁 위에 놓고 앉으세요.
12. 물을 한 모금 마시고 점심을 즐기세요.

18 Using the Vending Machine

A

1. You want to get a cup of coffee from the machine.
2. Take out some coins from your purse.
3. Go to the vending machine.
4. Insert your coins in the slot.
5. Lights come on the available items.
6. Press the button for the kind of coffee you want.
7. A paper cup comes down from the machine.
8. The machine fills the cup with coffee.
9. Now, the machine signals it's over.
10. Take the cup out of the machine.
11. Enjoy the coffee.
12. Are you finished?
13. Throw the empty cup into the collection box.

Key Vocabulary

- take out: 끄집어내다
- insert: 끼워넣다
- Lights come on: 불이 들어오다
- paper cup: 종이컵
- come down: 내려오다
- signal: 신호, 신호를 보내다
- take A out of B: A를 B에서 끄집어내다
- throw A into B: A를 B 속으로 버리다
- vending machine: 자동판매기
- slot: 동전구멍
- available items: 가능한(팔 수 있는) 항목들
- fill A with B: A를 B로 채우다
- It's over: 끝나다.
- Are you finished?: 끝났습니까?
- empty cup: 빈 컵
- collection box: 수집함

B

1. You want to get a cup of coffee ________ the machine.
2. Take out some ________ from your purse.
3. Go to the __________ machine.
4. _________ your coins in the slot.

5. Lights come on the available _________.
6. Press the button ______ the kind of coffee you want.
7. A paper cup comes ________ from the machine.
8. The machine _________ the cup with coffee.

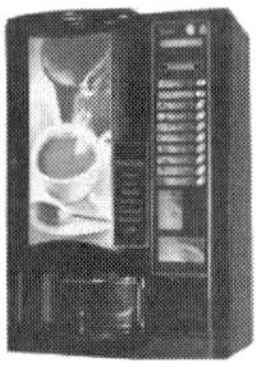

9. Now, the machine signals it's ________.
10. Take the cup _______ of the machine.
11. Enjoy the coffee.
12. _______ you finished?
13. Throw the _________ cup into the collection box.

C

1. 당신은 기계에서 커피를 한 잔 뽑고 싶습니다.
2. 지갑에서 동전을 몇 개 끄집어내세요.
3. 자동판매기로 가세요.
4. 동전구멍에 동전들을 넣으세요.
5. 가능한 항목에 불이 들어옵니다.
6. 당신이 원하는 종류의 커피 버튼을 누르세요.
7. 기계에서 종이컵이 내려옵니다.
8. 기계가 컵을 커피로 채웁니다.
9. 자, 끝났다고 기계가 알려줍니다.
10. 기계에서 컵을 끄집어내세요.
11. 커피를 즐기세요.
12. 다 마셨습니까?
13. 빈 컵은 수집함에 버리세요.

19 A Pay Day

A

1. Today is your pay day.
2. Go to the bank with your bankbook and a picture ID.
3. It's crowded. Pick up the waiting number.
4. While waiting, put your bankbook into a bank machine and check the balance.

5. Fill in the withdraw slip, sit and wait.
6. Finally, your number lights up.

7. Go to the window and give the teller the withdraw slip, bankbook and your ID.
8. The teller asks you how you want your money.
9. Tell him/her that you want all in cash.
10. The teller gives you the money in cash and returns your bankbook and ID.

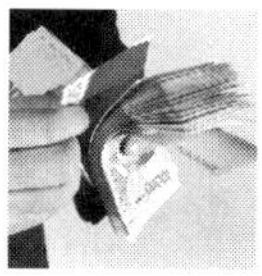

11. Take all of them. Say "Thank you!" and leave.

Key Vocabulary

- pay day: 봉급날
- bankbook: 은행통장
- picture ID(identification): 사진이 있는 신분증
- waiting number: 대기번호
- pick up: 뽑다
- put A into B: A를 B속에 집어넣다
- check the balance: 잔고를 확인하다
- fill in: 기록하다, 써넣다
- withdraw slip: 출금청구서
- return: 돌려주다
- in cash: 현금으로
- take all of them: 모두 다 가지다.

B

1. Today is your ______ day.
2. Go to the bank with your bankbook and a _________ ID.
3. It's crowded. _______ up the waiting number.

4. While waiting, put your bankbook into a bank machine and check the __________.
5. Fill in the ___________ slip, sit and wait.

6. Finally, your number ___________ up.
7. Go to the window and give the ________ the withdraw slip, bankbook and your ID.
8. The teller asks you _________ you want your money.
9. Tell him/her that you want all in _________.

10. The teller gives you the money _____ cash and __________ your bankbook and ID.
11. _________ all of them. Say "Thank you!" and leave.

C

1. 오늘은 당신의 봉급날입니다.
2. 통장과 사진이 있는 신분증을 가지고 은행으로 가세요.
3. 복잡합니다. 대기번호를 뽑으세요.
4. 기다리는 동안 은행 기계에 통장을 넣고 잔고가 얼마인지 확인하세요.
5. 출금청구서에 기록을 하고 앉아서 기다리세요.
6. 마침내 당신의 대기번호가 켜졌습니다.
7. 창구로 가서 은행원에게 출금청구서와 통장과 신분증을 주세요.
8. 은행원이 당신에게 돈을 어떻게 드릴지 묻습니다.
9. 모두 현금으로 달라고 말하세요.
10. 은행원이 당신에게 돈을 현금으로 주고, 통장과 신분증을 돌려줍니다.
11. 모두 다 가지고 "감사합니다!"라고 말하고 떠나세요.

20 Using the Microwave Oven

A

1. You brought your lunch today.
2. You need to warm it up.
3. Go to the kitchen.

4. Unwrap your lunch and put the food in a container.
5. The container must be for the microwave oven.
6. Now, open the microwave oven.
7. Set the timer for two minutes.
8. Press the start button and wait.
9. The bell rings. It's done.

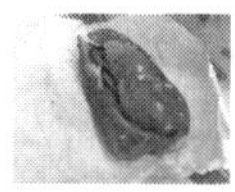

10. Open the door and take out the food.
11. What a good smell!
12. Take a sip of water and enjoy the food.

Key Vocabulary

- bring/brought: 가져오다/가져왔다
- warm up: 데우다
- unwrap: (포장을) 풀다
- container: 용기
- microwave oven: 전자레인지
- set the timer for 2 minutes: 타이머를 2분에 맞추다.
- press: 누르다
- ring: 벨이 울리다
- It's done: 다 되었다.
- take out: 꺼내다
- What a good smell!: 냄새 좋다!
- take a sip of water: 물 한 모금 마시다.

B

1. You brought your lunch today.
2. You need to ________ it up.
3. Go to the kitchen.

4. __________ your lunch and put the food in a container.
5. The ______________ must be for the microwave oven.
6. Now, open the microwave oven.
7. _________ the timer for two minutes.

8. ___________ the start button and wait.
9. The bell rings. It's _________.
10. Open the door and __________ out the food.
11. __________ a good smell!

12. Take a _________ of water and enjoy the food.

C

1. 당신은 오늘 점심을 가져왔습니다.
2. 당신은 그것을 데워야 합니다.
3. 부엌으로 가세요.
4. 점심 포장을 벗기고 용기에 음식을 담으세요.
5. 용기는 전자레인지용이어야 합니다.
6. 자, 전자레인지를 여세요.
7. 시간을 2분으로 맞추세요.
8. 시작버튼을 누르고 기다리세요.
9. 벨이 울립니다. 다 됐습니다.
10. 문을 열고 음식을 꺼내세요.
11. 냄새가 좋아요!
12. 물 한 모금 마시고 음식을 즐기세요.

21 Making a Copy

A

1. You need to make some copies of your document.
2. Go to the copy machine.
3. Turn on the machine and wait during the warm-up.
4. Finally, the machine signals it's ready.
5. Open the top of the machine.
6. Put your document face down.
7. Close the top and press the number of copies you want.
8. Press the start button.
9. The machine starts working.
10. It's done. Take the copies.
11. Open the top and take the document.
12. Close the top and go back to your desk.

Key Vocabulary

- make a copy: 복사하다
- copy machine: 복사기
- turn on: 켜다
- warm-up: 예열
- signal: 신호를 보내다
- ready: 준비된
- close the top: 뚜껑을 닫다
- put ~ face down: ~을 엎어놓다
- press: 누르다
- the number of copies: 복사물의 장 수
- start working: 작동하기 시작하다
- It's done: 다 됐다.
- take: 가지다, 챙기다
- go back to ~: ~로 돌아가다

B

1. You need to make some ________ of your document.
2. Go to the ________ machine.
3. Turn _____ the machine and wait during the _________.
4. Finally, the machine signals it's _________.

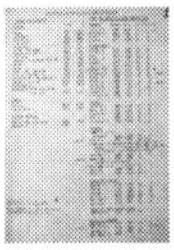

5. Open the _______ of the machine.
6. Put your document face ________.
7. Close the top and _________ the number of copies you want.

8. Press the _________ button.
9. The machine starts ___________.
10. It's ________. Take the copies.
11. Open the top and _______ the document.
12. Close the ________ and go back to your desk.

C

1. 당신은 서류 몇 장을 복사해야 합니다.
2. 복사기로 가세요.
3. 기계를 켜고 예열이 되는 동안 기다리세요.
4. 마침내 준비되었다고 기계가 신호를 보냅니다.
5. 기계의 뚜껑을 여세요.
6. 서류를 엎어서 놓으세요.
7. 두껑을 닫고 원하는 복사물 수를 누르세요.
8. 시작 버튼을 누리세요.
9. 기계가 작동하기 시작합니다.
10. 다 됐습니다. 복사물을 챙기세요.
11. 뚜껑을 열고 서류를 챙기세요.
12. 뚜껑을 닫고 자리로 돌아가세요.

22 Working Overtime

A

1. You have tons of work to finish by tomorrow.
2. You can't leave the office until you get it done.
3. Keep working on it.
4. You already passed the closing time.
5. You feel tired. Drink some coffee.
6. Then, the phone rings.
7. Pick up the phone. It's your mom.
8. She asks you when you are off.
9. Tell her that you have to work till late.
10. She asks you to have dinner first.
11. She always worries about your health.
12. Tell her that you will do as you are told.
13. Say "I love you, mom!" and hang up the phone.

Key Vocabulary

- tons of work: 대단히 많은 일 ◆ by tomorrow: 내일까지
- until you get it done: 그것을 완성할 때까지
- keep working: 계속해서 일하다
- pass the closing time: 퇴근시간을 넘기다
- The phone rings: 전화가 울리다.
- pick up the phone: 전화를 받다.
- be off: 퇴근하다 ◆ till late: 늦게까지
- worry about ~: ~에 대해 걱정하다
- as you are told: 들은 대로, 시키는 대로
- hang up the phone: 전화를 끊다.

B

1. You have tons of work to finish _____ tomorrow.
2. You can't leave the office ________ you get it done.
3. Keep ___________ on it.
4. You already passed the __________ time.
5. You feel tired. Drink some coffee.

6. Then, the phone ___________.
7. __________ up the phone. It's your mom.

8. She asks you when you are _______.
9. Tell her that you have to work ______ late.
10. She asks you ______ have dinner first.
11. She always ___________ about your health.
12. Tell her that you will do ______ you are told.
13. Say "I love you, mom!" and _________ up the phone.

C

1. 당신은 내일까지 끝내야 할 일이 대단히 많습니다.
2. 완성할 때까지 퇴근할 수 없습니다.
3. 계속 일을 하세요.
4. 당신은 이미 퇴근시간을 넘겼습니다.
5. 당신은 피곤합니다. 커피를 좀 마시세요.
6. 그때 전화가 울립니다.
7. 전화를 받으세요. 당신의 어머니이군요.
8. 그녀가 언제 퇴근인지 묻습니다.
9. 늦게까지 일해야 한다고 말씀드리세요.
10. 저녁 먼저 먹으라고 말씀하십니다.
11. 그녀는 항상 당신 건강을 걱정하십니다.
12. 시키는 대로 하겠다고 말씀드리세요.
13. “사랑해요, 엄마!”라고 말하고 전화를 끊으세요.

23 Taking a Message

A

1. The phone is ringing in the office.
2. Everyone is busy working and nobody answers the phone.
3. You run to the phone and answer the phone.
4. The caller asks for one of your colleagues.
5. Tell the caller he/she is not in.

6. The caller asks when he/she will be back.
7. Tell the caller that he/she will be available late in the afternoon.
8. The caller asks if you can take the message.
9. Say "Sure. go ahead." and take the message.
10. Put the message on your colleague's desk.

11. Later, your colleague comes back and gets the message.

Key Vocabulary

- The phone is ringing: 전화벨이 울리다.
- be busy ~ing: ~하느라 바쁘다
- ask for~: ~을 요구하다, 원하다
- colleague: 직장동료
- in: 안에 있는
- available: 가능한, 쓸 수 있는, 만날 수 있는, 통화할 수 있는
- late in the afternoon: 오후 늦게
- take the message: 전달사항을 받다
- go ahead: 계속하다, 나아가다

B

1. The phone is __________ in the office.
2. Everyone is __________ working and nobody answers the phone.

3. You run _____ the phone and answer the phone.
4. The caller asks _______ one of your colleagues.
5. Tell the caller he/she is not _____.
6. The caller asks when he/she will be back.
7. Tell the caller that he/she will be ___________ late in the afternoon.
8. The caller asks if you can _________ the message.

9. Say “Sure. go ___________.” and take the message.
10. Put the message _____ your colleague's desk.
11. Later, your colleague comes _________ and gets the message.

C

1. 사무실에서 전화가 울립니다.
2. 모두 일하느라 바쁘고 아무도 전화를 받지 않습니다.
3. 당신이 전화기로 달려가서 전화를 받습니다.
4. 전화를 건 사람이 동료 중 한 사람을 찾습니다.
5. 그는 지금 사무실에 없다고 말하세요.
6. 전화 건 사람이 그가 언제 돌아오느냐고 묻습니다.
7. 오후 늦게 통화가 가능하다고 말하세요.
8. 메시지를 받아줄 수 있겠느냐고 묻습니다.
9. “물론입니다. 어서 말씀하세요.”라고 말하고 메시지를 받으세요.
10. 메시지를 동료의 책상 위에 올려놓습니다.
12. 나중에 동료가 돌아와서 메시지를 봅니다.

24 In the Office

A

1. You are a man working in an office.
2. You feel exhausted and want to relax.
3. Sit at your desk and loosen your tie.
4. Unbutton your jacket and take it off.
5. Roll up your sleeves and untie your shoes.
6. Put your legs on the desk.
7. Uh-oh! Here comes the boss!
8. Put down your legs from the desk.
9. Tighten your tie.
10. Put on your jacket and button it up.
11. Put on your shoes and tie them.
12. Get to work and say "Hello." to the boss.

Key Vocabulary

- exhausted: 지친, 무척 피곤한
- relax: 쉬다. 휴식하다
- loosen: 느슨하게 풀다
- unbutton: 단추를 풀다
- roll up/roll down: 위로 감아올리다/아래로 풀어내리다
- tie/untie: 묶다, 매다/ 풀다
- Here comes ~: ~가 온다
- Put down A from B: A를 B에서 내리다
- tighten: 바짝 매다
- button up: 단추를 끝까지 채우다
- put on: 입다, 신다
- get to work: 일을 시작하다

B

1. You are a man working in an office.
2. You feel exhausted and want to ________.
3. Sit at your desk and ________ your tie.
4. ________ your jacket and take it ______.
5. Roll ______ your sleeves and ________ your shoes.
6. Put your legs ______ the desk.
7. Uh-oh! ________ comes the boss!
8. Put ________ your legs from the desk.
9. ________ your tie.
10. ________ on your jacket and ________ it up.
11. Put on your shoes and ________ them.
12. Get to ________ and say "Hello." to the boss.

C

1. 당신은 사무실에서 일하는 남자입니다.
2. 당신은 피곤해서 쉬고 싶습니다.
3. 책상에 앉아서 넥타이를 느슨하게 하세요.
4. 상의의 단추를 풀고 옷을 벗으세요.
5. 소매를 걷어 올리고 구두끈을 푸세요.
6. 다리를 책상 위에 올리세요.
7. 아이고! 상사가 오시네요!
8. 책상에서 다리를 내리세요.
9. 넥타이를 매세요.
10. 상의를 입고 단추를 잠그세요.
11. 구두를 신고 끈을 묶으세요.
12. 일을 시작하세요. 그리고 상사께 "안녕하세요?"라고 말하세요.

25 Taking a Day Off

A

1. You stayed in your office till late last night.
2. You don't feel well this morning.
3. You feel dizzy and ache all over.
4. You'd better stay at home today.

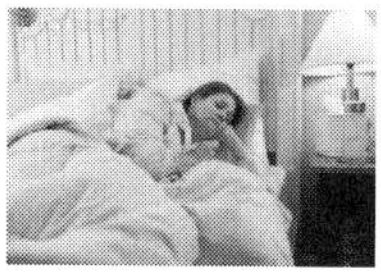

5. Call your company and a colleague answers the phone.
6. Inform that you are sick and want to take a day off.
7. Your colleague says "Take it easy.
   Let me tell the boss about it."
8. Say "Thank you!" and hang up the phone.
9. Take some medicine for your symptom.

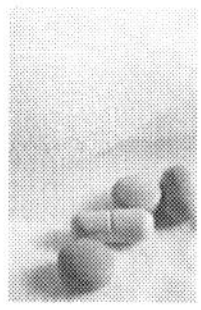

10. Lie down in your bed and take more sleep.

Key Vocabulary

- feel well: 건강하게 느끼다
- feel dizzy: 어지러움을 느끼다
- ache all over: 온몸이 쑤시다, 몸살이 나다
- had(='d) better~: ~하는 게 낫다
- company: 회사
- colleague: 동료
- inform: 알리다, 정보를 제공하다
- take a day off: 하루를 쉬다
- take it easy: 편히 쉬다.
- Let me ~ : ~하겠습니다.
- hang up the phone: 전화를 끊다.
- symptom: 증세
- lie down: 눕다

B

1. You stayed in your office _______ late last night.
2. You don't feel _______ this morning.
3. You feel _______ and ache all _____.
4. You'd ________ stay at home today.

5. Call your company and a __________ answers the phone.
6. ___________ that you are sick and want to take a day ___________.
7. Your colleague says "Take it _______. ______ me tell the boss about it."
8. Say "Thank you!" and _______ up the phone.
9. ________ some medicine for your symptom.
10. _______ down in your bed and take more sleep.

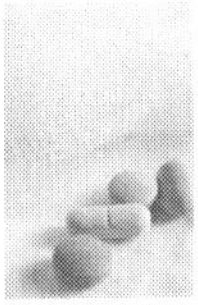

C

1. 당신은 지난밤 늦게까지 사무실에 있었어요.
2. 오늘 아침 몸이 좋지 않습니다.
3. 어지럽고 온몸이 쑤십니다.
4. 오늘 집에 있는 게 낫겠습니다.
5. 회사에 전화를 하니 동료가 전화를 받습니다.
6. 몸이 아프다고 알리고 하루를 쉬고 싶다고 하세요.
7. 동료가 말합니다. "편히 쉬세요. 사장님께 얘기할게요."
8. "감사합니다!"라고 말하고 전화를 끊으세요.
9. 증세에 좋은 약을 좀 드세요.
10. 침대에 누워서 잠을 좀더 자세요.

26 Making a Presentation

A

1. You have to make a presentation at a conference.
2. You need to check the facilities first.
3. Go into the conference room.
4. The computer and the beam projector are already on.
5. Insert your USB in the computer.
6. Check if your file for the presentation is OK.

7. Good! Everything looks fine.
8. The conference room is full of audience.

9. Finally, it's time to start.
10. The modulator introduces you to the audience.
11. Say "Thank you!" for the introduction and start your presentation.
12. Don't forget to keep the time limit!

Key Vocabulary

- make a presentation: 발표하다.
- at a conference: 회의(장)에서
- facilities: 시설
- USB(Universal Serial Bus): 범용직렬버스
  –컴퓨터와 주변 기기를 연결하는 데 쓰이는 입출력 표준 가운데 하나
  ※ bus: (컴퓨터) 버스, 데이터원(源)
- insert A in B: A를 B에 끼우다.
- check if ~: ~인지 확인하다
- full of ~: ~로 가득 찬
- audience: 청중
- modulator: 사회자
- Don't forget to ~: ~하는 것 잊지 마세요.
- keep the time limit: 시간제한을 지키다

B

1. You have to ________ a presentation at a conference.
2. You need to check the _______________ first.
3. Go __________ the conference room.
4. The computer and the beam projector are already _____.
5. ____________ your USB in the computer.
6. Check ________ your file for the presentation is OK.

7. Good! Everything __________ fine.

8. The conference room is full of ______.
9. Finally, it's time ______ start.
10. The _____________ introduces you to the audience.
11. Say "Thank you!" ______ the introduction and start your presentation.
12. Don't forget to _______ the time limit!

C

1. 당신은 오늘 회의에서 발표를 해야합니다.
2. 당신은 시설을 먼저 점검할 필요가 있습니다.
3. 회의장으로 들어가세요.
4. 컴퓨터와 빔프로젝터는 이미 켜져 있습니다.
5. 당신의 USB를 컴퓨터에 끼우세요.
6. 발표할 파일이 정상인지 확인하세요.
7. 좋아요! 모든 게 괜찮아 보입니다.
8. 회의장이 청중으로 가득 찼네요.
9. 마침내 시작할 시각입니다.
10. 사회자가 청중에게 당신을 소개합니다.
11. 소개에 대해 "감사합니다."라고 말하고 발표를 시작하세요.
12. 시간제한 지키는 것 잊지 마세요!

27 Leaving for Home

A

1. It's about time for you to leave the office.
2. Wrap up your work.
3. Take your USB out of the computer and put it in your bag.
4. Turn off the computer.
5. Clean your desk and empty the trash can.
6. Call home and inform your family that you are leaving the office.
7. Put the answering machine on.
8. Put on your coat and pick up your bag.
9. Make sure all the switches are off.
10. Good! Everything looks fine.
11. Lock the door and leave for home.

Key Vocabulary

- wrap up: 끝내다
- take A out of B: A를 B에서 끄집어내다
- turn off: 끄다
- empty: 비우다
- inform: 알리다
- put on: 켜다, 입다
- pick up: 집어 들다
- make sure~: ~하도록 하라, ~를 명심하다
- be off: 꺼지다
- leave for~: ~을 향해서 떠나다

B

1. It's about time ________ you to leave the office.
2. _________ up your work.
3. Take your USB ______ of the computer and put it in your bag.
4. Turn ________ the computer.
5. Clean your desk and __________ the trash can.
6. Call home and inform your family that you are _____ the office.
7. Put the answering machine _____.
8. _____ on your coat and _______ up your bag.
9. Make _______ all the switches are off.
10. Good! Everything looks fine.
11. ________ the door and leave _______ home.

C

1. 퇴근할 시간입니다.
2. 일을 끝내세요.
3. 컴퓨터에서 USB를 빼서 가방 속에 넣으세요.
4. 컴퓨터를 끄세요.
5. 책상을 정돈하고 쓰레기통을 비우세요.
6. 집에 전화를 걸어 가족에게 지금 퇴근한다고 말하세요.
7. 응답기를 켜세요.
8. 코트를 입고 가방을 집으세요.
9. 모든 스위치가 꺼졌는지 확인하세요.
10. 좋습니다. 모든 게 잘 됐습니다.
11. 문을 잠그고 집을 향해 떠나세요.

28 Sharpening the Pencil

A

1. You feel the point of your pencil. It is dull.
2. You need to sharpen your pencil but you don't have a pencil sharpener.
3. Borrow a pencil sharpener from your colleague.
4. Stick the pencil in the hole and sharpen it.
5. Take the pencil out of the hole.
6. Feel the point. Ouch! It's sharp!
7. Write some words on the paper.
8. Oops! the point has been broken.
9. Sharpen the pencil again.
   Don't break the point this time!
10. Clean the pencil sharpener.
11. Return it to your colleague and say "Thank you!".

Key Vocabulary

- feel: 만져보다
- point: 끝의 뾰족한 부분
- dull: 무딘
- sharpen: 깎다, 날카롭게 만들다
- pencil sharpener: 연필깎이
- stick A in B: A를 B 속에 끼우다.
- take A out of B: A를 B에서 빼내다
- broken: 부러진
- break: 부러뜨리다
- this time: 이번에는
- clean: 청소하다
- return: 돌려주다 (=give back)

B

1. You feel the point of your pencil. It is ________.
2. You need to ________ your pencil but you don't have a pencil sharpener.
3. ________ a pencil sharpener from your colleague.
4. Stick the pencil in the hole and __________ it.
5. Take the pencil _____ of the hole.
6. Feel the point. Ouch! It's _______!
7. Write some words on the paper.
8. Oops! the point has been ________.
9. Sharpen the pencil again.
   Don't ________ the point this time!
10. __________ the pencil sharpener.
11. __________ it to your colleague and say "Thank you!".

C

1. 당신은 연필 끝을 만져봅니다. 무디네요.
2. 당신은 연필을 깎아야 하는데 연필깎이가 없습니다.
3. 동료에게서 연필깎이를 빌리세요.
4. 연필을 구멍 속에다 넣고 깎으세요.
5. 구멍에서 연필을 빼내세요.
6. 끝을 만져보세요. 아야! 날카롭습니다!
7. 종이 위에 몇 자 적어보세요.
8. 아이고! 연필 끝이 부러졌습니다.
9. 연필을 다시 깎으세요. 이번에는 심을 부러뜨리지 마세요!
10. 연필깎이를 청소하세요.
11. 그것을 동료에게 돌려주면서 “고마워요”라고 말하세요.

29 Talking to a Colleague

A

1. You have a colleague who makes a lot of noise.
2. You want to let her know.
3. Ask her if she has time to have a cup of coffee.

4. She says, "Sure!"
5. Go to the lounge with her.
6. Get two cups of coffee from the vending machine.
7. Sit down and drink the coffee.
8. Tell her that you have something to ask for.

9. She says, "Sure! Go ahead."

10. Tell her to lower her voice when she is on the phone.
11. She is embarrassed and says, "Oh, I'm so sorry! I didn't know that I was making noise!"
12. Tell her that you are sorry to have to say that.

Key Vocabulary

- make noise: 시끄럽게 굴다, 소란피우다
- a lot of: 많은
- noise: 소음
- let her know: 그녀가 알게 하다
- ask if ~: ~인지 묻다
- vending machine: 자동판매기
- ask for: 요구하다, 부탁하다
- go ahead: 계속하다, 그렇게 하다
- lower one's voice: (~의) 목소리를 낮추다
- be embarrassed: 당황하다

B

1. You have a colleague who __________ a lot of noise.
2. You want to _______ her know.
3. Ask her _______ she has time to have a cup of coffee.

4. She says, "__________!"
5. Go to the lounge with her.
6. Get two cups of coffee from the ___________ machine.
7. Sit down and drink the coffee.

8. Tell her that you have something _____ ask for.
9. She says, "Sure! Go __________."
10. Tell her to __________ her voice when she is ______ the phone.
11. She is ____________ and says, "Oh, I'm so sorry! I didn't know that I was making ___________!"
12. Tell her that you are sorry ______ have to say that.

C

1. 시끄럽게 구는 동료가 있습니다.
2. 그녀에게 알리고 싶습니다.
3. 그녀에게 커피 한 잔 할 시간 있느냐고 물어보세요.
4. "물론이죠!"라고 그녀가 말합니다.
5. 그녀와 함께 휴게실로 가세요.
6. 자동판매기에서 커피 두 잔을 빼세요.
7. 앉아서 커피를 마십니다.
8. 부탁할 게 있다고 그녀에게 말하세요.
9. "물론이죠! 어서 말하세요."라고 그녀가 말합니다.
10. 전화할 때 목소리를 낮춰달라고 말하세요.
11. 그녀가 당황해서 말합니다. "아, 정말 미안합니다. 내가 시끄럽게 구는 줄 몰랐어요!"
12. 당신도 그렇게 말할 수밖에 없어서 미안하다고 말하세요.

SECTION 3

Health & Leisure

30 Washing Your Hands

A

1. You just came back home from outside.
2. You need to wash your hands first.
3. Go into the bathroom.
4. Turn on the water.
5. Pick up the soap.
6. Wash your hands.
7. Put the soap down.
8. Rinse your hands.
9. Turn off the water.
10. Pick up the towel from the towel rack.
11. Dry your hands with the towel.
12. Put the towel back on the rack.
13. Put some lotion on your hands and rub it.

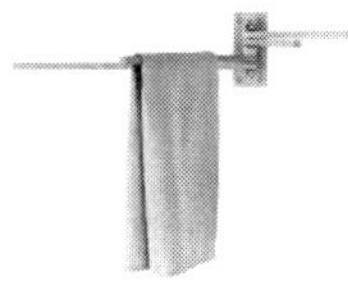

Key Vocabulary

- come back from ~: ~에서 돌아오다
- turn on: 틀다
- pick up: 집어 들다
- put down: 내려놓다
- rinse: 헹구다
- turn off: 끄다, 잠그다
- towel rack: 수건걸이
- dry: 닦다, 말리다
- put back: 도로 두다
- put lotion on ~: ~에 로션을 바르다 (put on: 바르다)
- rub: 문지르다

B

1. You just came back home from ________.
2. You need to ______ your hands first.
3. Go _______ the bathroom.
4. _______ on the water.
5. ________up the soap.
6. Wash your hands.
7. Put the soap ________.
8. _______ your hands.
9. Turn ______ the water.
10. Pick up the towel from the towel ________.
11. ______ your hands with the towel.
12. Put the towel ________ on the rack.
13. Put some lotion _____ your hands and ______ it.

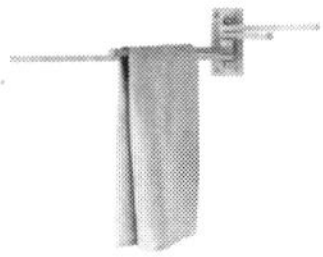

C

1. 당신은 밖에서 집으로 막 돌아왔습니다.
2. 손부터 먼저 씻어야 합니다.
3. 욕실로 들어가세요.
4. 물을 트세요.
5. 비누를 집으세요.
6. 손을 씻으세요.
7. 비누를 내려놓으세요.
8. 손을 헹구세요.
9. 물을 끄세요.
10. 수건걸이에서 수건을 집으세요.
11. 수건으로 손을 닦으세요.
12. 수건을 걸이에 도로 놓으세요.
13. 손에 로션을 좀 바르고 문지르세요.

31 Putting Drops in Your eyes

A

1. You're going to put drops in your eyes.
2. Open the bottle of eye drops.

3. Fill the dropper.
4. Put your head back and open your eyes wide.
5. Keep them open.
6. Hold one eye open with your fingers.

7. Squeeze a drop into it.
8. Don't blink!
9. Oh, You missed it!
   The drop is running down your cheek.
10. Wipe it off and try again.
11. There! That's it. You did it.
12. Go ahead and blink now.

Key Vocabulary

- (eye) drop: 안약, 점안제
- dropper: 점적기, 드롭퍼
- open wide: 크게 뜨다
- squeeze A into B: A를 B 속으로 짜 넣다
- blink: 깜박이다
- wipe off: 닦아내다
- You did it: 해냈다.
- fill: 채우다
- put back: 뒤로 젖히다
- keep open: 계속 뜨고 있다
- miss: 놓치다
- cheek: 뺨
- run down: 흘러내리다
- That's it: 바로 그것이다.
- Go ahead and blink: 자아 깜박이세요.

B

1. You're going to _______ drops in your eyes.
2. Open the bottle of _______ drops.

3. ________ the dropper.
4. Put your head ________ and open your eyes ________.
5. Keep them open.
6. Hold one eye ________ with your fingers.

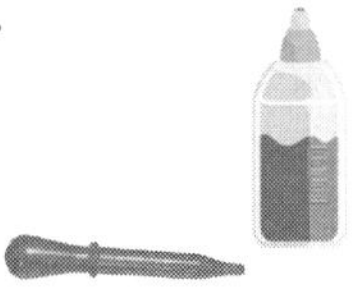

7. ____________ a drop into it.
8. Don't _________!
9. Oh, You ___________ it!
   The drop is running ________ your cheek.
10. __________ it off and try again.
11. There! That's it. You _______ it.
12. Go _________ and blink now.

C

1. 당신은 눈에 안약을 좀 넣으려고 합니다.
2. 안약 병을 여세요.
3. 드롭퍼를 채우세요.
4. 머리를 뒤로 젖히고 눈을 크게 뜨세요.
5. 계속 뜨고 있으세요.
6. 손가락으로 한쪽 눈을 벌리세요.
7. 안약을 한 방울 짜 넣으세요.
8. 눈을 깜박이지 마세요!
9. 아, 놓쳤습니다! 안약이 뺨을 타고 흘러내려요.
10. 닦아내고 다시 시도하세요.
11. 그렇죠! 바로 그것입니다. 당신은 해냈어요.
12. 자아 이제 눈을 깜박이세요.

32 Taking Vitamin Pills

A

1. You need to take care of yourself.
2. You decide to take some vitamins.
3. Pick up the bottle of vitamin pills.
4. Take the top off and take out a pill.
5. Put the top back on.

6. Put the bottle down.
7. Put the pill in your mouth.
8. Drink some water and swallow the pill.

9. Uh-oh! It's stuck in your throat!
10. Drink some more water.
11. O.K. Good! This time, it went down.
12. Be careful next time!

Key Vocabulary

- take care of ~: ~을 돌보다
- pick up: 집어 들다, 집다
- take off: 열다, 벗기다
- top: 두껑
- put A in B: A를 B에 넣다
- swallow: 삼키다
- It's stuck in ~: ~에 걸렸다.
- go down: 내려가다
- next time: 다음번에
- take: (약을) 먹다
- bottle of vitamin pills: 비타민 알약이 든 병
- put ~ back on: ~을 도로 씌우다, 닫다
- Uh-oh!: 아이고! 이런!
- throat: 목, 식도
- Be careful.: 조심하세요.

B

1. You need to ________ care of yourself.
2. You decide to ________ some vitamins.
3. Pick ______ the bottle of vitamin pills.
4. Take the ________ off and ________ out a pill.
5. Put the top back _______.
6. Put the bottle __________.
7. ________ the pill in your mouth.
8. Drink some water and ___________ the pill.
9. Uh-oh! It's _________ in your throat!
10. Drink some more water.
11. O.K. Good! This time, it went _________.
12. Be ______________ next time!

C

1. 당신은 몸을 돌볼 필요가 있습니다.
2. 당신은 비타민을 먹기로 결정했습니다.
3. 비타민 병을 집으세요.
4. 뚜껑을 열고 알약을 하나 끄집어내세요.
5. 뚜껑을 도로 닫으세요.
6. 병을 내려놓으세요.
7. 알약을 입에 넣으세요.
8. 물을 마시고 알약을 삼키세요.
9. 아이고, 약이 목에 걸렸네요!
10. 물을 좀더 마시세요.
11. 네, 좋습니다. 이번에는 내려갔어요.
12. 다음번엔 조심하세요!

33 Doctor's Appointment

A

1. You have a doctor's appointment.
2. Go to the clinic.
3. Tell the receptionist your name and the appointment time.
4. Have a seat and wait.
5. You're nervous but try to be calm.
6. Finally! Here comes the nurse.
7. Follow her into the examination room.
8. Say "Hello." to the doctor and sit down.
9. The doctor examines your body with the stethoscope.
10. He asks you to stick out your tongue and say, "Ah".
11. He says you're fine. What a relief!

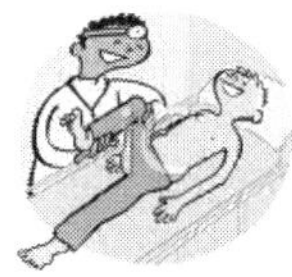

Key Vocabulary

- appointment: (시간)약속 (cf. promise: 맹세, 약속)
- clinic: 개인병원 (cf. hospital: 종합병원)
- receptionist: 접수원
- nervous: 떨리는, 긴장되는
- calm: 태연한, 평온한
- follow A into B: A를 따라 B로 들어가다
- examination room: 진찰실
- stethoscope: 청진기
- stick out: 내밀다
- relief: 안심

B

1. You have a doctor's ________________.
2. Go to the clinic.
3. Tell the __________ your name and the appointment time.
4. _________ a seat and wait.
5. You're __________ but try to be calm.

6. Finally! Here ___________ the nurse.
7. Follow her into the _____________ room.
8. Say "Hello." _____ the doctor and sit down.

9. The doctor _____________ your body with thestethoscope.
10. He asks you to _______ out your tongue and say, "Ah".
11. He says you're fine. What a ____________!

C

1. 당신은 의사와 약속이 있습니다.
2. 병원으로 가세요.
3. 접수원에게로 가서 이름과 약속시간을 말하세요.
4. 앉아서 기다리세요.
5. 당신은 떨리지만 태연하려고 애씁니다.
6. 마침내! 간호사가 옵니다.
7. 그녀를 따라 진찰실로 가세요.
8. 의사에게 "안녕하세요."라고 인사하고 앉으세요.
9. 의사는 청진기로 당신의 몸을 진찰합니다.
10. 그는 당신에게 혀를 내밀고 "아"하라고 합니다.
11. 그는 당신이 괜찮다고 합니다. 정말 안심이네요!

34 You're Getting Sick

A

1. You have a splitting headache and a runny nose.
2. You also sneeze and cough.
3. Cover your nose and sneeze.
4. Cover your mouth and cough.
5. Blow your nose with the tissue paper.
6. Oh, it looks serious.
7. Leave the house and go to the drugstore.
8. Oh, you feel dizzy.
9. Lean against the wall for a while.
10. Go into the drugstore.
11. Buy some aspirin and some drinks for cold.
12. Go back home and take care of yourself.

Key Vocabulary

- splitting headache: 쪼개는 듯 심한 두통
- runny nose: 콧물이 나는 코
- sneeze: 재채기하다
- cough: 기침하다
- cover: 막다, 덮다
- blow one's nose: 코를 풀다
- tissue paper: 휴지
- look serious: 심각해 보이다
- leave: 떠나다
- drugstore: 약국(상비약을 포함해서 생활용품을 파는 가게)
- dizzy: 어지러운
- lean against~: ~에 기대다
- for a while: 잠깐
- take care of ~: ~을 돌보다

B

1. You have a __________ headache and a ________ nose.
2. You also sneeze and cough.
3. Cover your nose and __________.
4. Cover your mouth and _________.
5. _______ your nose with the tissue paper.
6. Oh, it looks _______.
7. _________ the house and go to the drugstore.
8. Oh, you feel _________.
9. Lean ________ the wall for a while.
10. Go into the drugstore.
11. Buy some aspirin and some drinks ______ cold.
12. Go back home and _______ care of yourself.

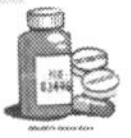

C

1. 당신은 머리가 쪼개지는 듯 심하게 아프고 콧물이 납니다.
2. 당신은 또한 재채기도하고 기침도 합니다.
3. 코를 막고 재채기를 하세요.
4. 입을 막고 기침을 하세요.
5. 화장지로 코를 푸세요.
6. 아, 심각해 보입니다.
7. 집을 떠나 약국으로 가세요.
8. 아, 당신은 어지럽습니다.
9. 잠시 벽에 기대세요.
10. 약국으로 들어가세요.
11. 아스피린과 감기에 좋은 드링크를 좀 사세요.
12. 집으로 돌아가서 몸조리하세요.

35 Bleeding

A

1. You are walking down the street.
2. Fall down and skin your knee and scream.
3. Get up and cry. It hurts so much!
4. Look at your knee. It's bleeding!
5. Put your handkerchief on it.
6. Limp to the drugstore.
7. Buy some iodine and bandaids.
8. Limp home.
9. Wash the wound.
10. Put some iodine on it.
11. Ow! It stings! Blow on it.
12. Unwrap a bandaid and put it over the wound.
13. Throw away the wrapper.

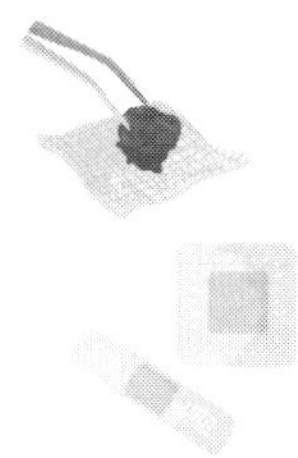

Key Vocabulary

- walk down the street: 길을 따라 걸어(내려)가다
- fall down: 넘어지다
- scream: 소리 지르다
- get up: 일어나다
- look at: 보다
- limp to ~; ~로 절뚝거리며 가다
- bandaid: 반창고
- wound: 상처
- It stings!: 아야! 아프다!
- unwrap: 포장을 뜯다, 풀다
- throw away: 버리다
- skin the knee: 무릎이 벗겨지다
- It hurts: 아프다.
- bleeding: 피나는, 피 흘리는
- iodine: 요오드
- limp home: 집으로 절뚝거리며 가다
- blow on ~: ~을 불다
- put A over B: A로 B 위를 덮다
- wrapper: 포장지

B

1. You are walking ________ the street.
2. Fall down and ________ your knee and scream.
3. Get ______ and cry. It ________ so much!
4. Look ____ your knee. It's _________!
5. Put your handkerchief _____ it.
6. ________ to the drugstore.
7. Buy some iodine and _________.
8. Limp _________.
9. Wash the _________.
10. _______ some iodine on it.
11. Ow! It _________! _______ on it.
12. _________ a bandaid and put it over the wound.
13. Throw away the __________.

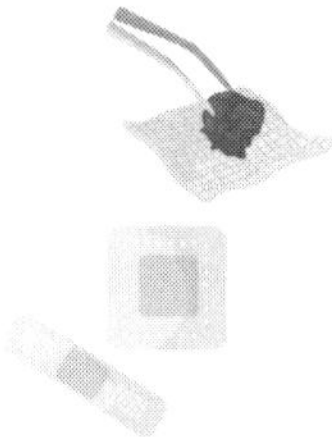

C

1. 당신은 길을 따라 걸어(내려)가고 있습니다.
2. 넘어져서 무릎이 벗겨지고 소리를 지르세요.
3. 일어나서 우세요. 너무 아파요!
4. 무릎을 보세요. 피가 나요!
5. 손수건을 갖다 대세요.
6. 약국으로 절뚝거리며 가세요.
7. 요오드와 반창고를 사세요.
8. 집으로 절뚝거리며 가세요.
9. 상처를 씻으세요.
10. 요오드를 바르세요.
11. 아, 아파요! 부세요.
12. 반창고를 뜯어서 상처 위에 붙이세요.
13. 포장지는 버리세요.

36 Calling an Ambulance

A

1. You slipped in the bathroom at night.
2. Your forehead hit the sink stand and is bleeding seriously.
3. Your family gives you first aid to stop the bleeding.
4. But the bleeding doesn't stop.
5. Call an ambulance.
6. The ambulance arrives in a few minutes.

7. The paramedic checks your wound and dresses it.
8. The ambulance takes you to the emergency room.
9. In the emergency room the doctor undresses and checks your wound.
10. The wound requires five stitches.
11. He sterilizes, anesthetizes, and stitches the wound.
12. What a night!

Key Vocabulary

- slip: 미끄러지다
- sink stand: 세면대
- seriously: 심하게
- in a few minutes: 몇 분 만에
- wound: 상처, 외상
- take A to B: A를 B로 데리고 가다
- stitch: (상처를) 꿰매기, 꿰매다
- sterilize: 소독하다
- forehead: 이마
- bleed: 피를 흘리다, 출혈하다
- first aid: 응급 처방
- paramedic: 응급구조원
- dress: 붕대를 감다
- emergency room: 응급실
- undress: 붕대를 풀다
- anesthetize: 마취시키다

B

1. You __________ in the bathroom at night.
2. Your ____________ hit the sink stand and is bleeding seriously.
3. Your family gives you first ______ to stop the bleeding.
4. But the bleeding doesn't _______.
5. Call an ___________.
6. The ambulance arrives ____ a few minutes.

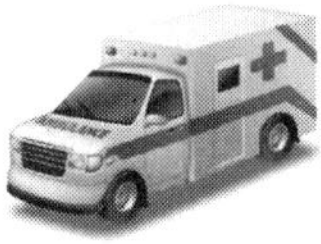

7. The __________ checks your wound and _________ it.
8. The ambulance takes you to the _____________ room.
9. In the emergency room the doctor _________ and checks your wound.
10. The wound requires five ____________.
11. He __________, ___________, and stitches the wound.
12. _________ a night!

C

1. 당신은 밤에 욕실에서 미끄러졌습니다.
2. 당신의 이마가 세면대에 부딪쳐서 출혈이 심합니다.
3. 가족이 출혈을 멈추기 위해 응급 처방을 합니다.
4. 하지만 출혈이 멈추지 않습니다.
5. 앰뷸런스를 부르세요.
6. 몇 분 안에 앰뷸런스가 도착합니다.
7. 응급구조원이 당신의 상처를 체크하고 붕대를 감습니다.
8. 앰뷸런스가 당신을 응급실로 데려갑니다.
9. 응급실에서 의사가 붕대를 풀고 상처를 체크합니다.
10. 다섯 바늘 꿰매야 하는 상처입니다.
11. 의사는 상처를 소독하고, 마취하고, 꿰맵니다.
12. 정말 별난 밤이군요!

37 At the Swimming Pool

A

1. You're at the swimming pool.
2. Put on your swim suit.
3. Stand at the edge of the pool.
4. Hold your nose and take a deep breath.
5. Jump in. (Splash!)
6. Swim across the pool.
7. Climb up the ladder and get out.
8. This time, go to the diving board.
9. Walk out over the water.
10. Dive into the water. Wonderful!
11. Hold your breath and swim underwater.
12. Now, swim to the surface and breathe hard.
13. You see your friend in front of you!
14. Splash your friend. Isn't it fun?

Key Vocabulary

- put on: 옷을 입다
- hold your nose: 코를 잡다
- jump in: 뛰어들다
- climb up: 올라가다
- swim across: 가로질러 헤엄치다
- diving board: 다이빙대
- dive into water: 물속으로 다이빙하다
- underwater: 물밑으로
- breathe hard: 크게 숨 쉬다
- splash: 튀다
- at the edge of ~: ~의 가장자리에
- take a deep breath: 깊은 숨을 쉬다
- get out: 나오다
- walk out over ~: ~위로 걸어 나오다
- hold breath: 숨을 멈추다
- to the surface: 표면으로
- in front of ~: ~앞에
- It is fun: 재미있다.

B

1. You're at the swimming pool.
2. Put on your swim ________.
3. Stand at the __________ of the pool.
4. ___________ your nose and take a _________ breath.
5. __________ in. (Splash!)
6. Swim _________ the pool.
7. _________ up the ladder and get out.
8. This time, go to the diving __________.

9. Walk out ________ the water.
10. Dive ________ the water. Wonderful!
11. Hold your ________ and swim __________.

12. Now, swim to the ____________ and breathe hard.
13. You see your friend in ___________ of you!
14. ___________ your friend. Isn't it ________?

C

1. 당신은 수영장에 있습니다.
2. 수영복을 입으세요.
3. 풀장 가장자리에 서세요.
4. 코를 잡고 숨을 깊게 들이쉬세요.
5. (물속으로)점프하세요. (풍덩!)
6. 풀장을 가로질러 헤엄치세요.
7. 사다리를 타고 올라 밖으로 나오세요.
8. 이번에는 다이빙대로 가세요.
9. 물 위쪽으로 걸어 나오세요.
10. 물속으로 다이빙하세요. 근사합니다!
11. 숨을 멈추고 물밑으로 헤엄치세요.
12. 이제 표면으로 헤엄치세요. 그리고 숨을 크게 쉬세요.
13. 당신 앞에 친구가 있네요.
14. 친구에게 물을 튀기세요. 재미있죠?

38 Taking a Walk

A

1. It's a beautiful Sunday afternoon and you want to take a walk.
2. You want to go to the park nearby.
3. Leave your house and walk on the sidewalk.

4. There's a traffic light over there.
5. Stop at the traffic light.
6. Wait until the light turns from red to green.
7. The light turns green. Cross the street by walking in the crosswalk.
8. After you cross the street, turn to your left.
9. Keep walking until you reach the underpass.
10. Finally, you are at the underpass.

11. Cross the street through the underpass.
12. When you get out of the underpass, you see the park in front of you.
13. Enjoy your afternoon at the park.

Key Vocabulary

- take a walk: 산책하다
- sidewalk: 인도
- traffic light: 신호등
- Turn to your left.: 왼쪽으로 돌다.
- until ~: ~할 때까지
- nearby: 근처
- over there: 저기, 저 너머
- cross the street: 길을 건너다
- keep ~ing: 계속해서 ~하다
- reach: 도달하다
- underpass: 지하도
- get out of ~: ~에서 나오다, 벗어나다
- in front of ~: ~앞에

B

1. It's a beautiful Sunday afternoon and you want to_____ a walk.
2. You want to go to the park __________.
3. Leave your house and walk on the ______.
4. There's a ___________ light over there.

5. ________ at the traffic light.
6. Wait _________ the light turns from red ___ green.
7. The light turns green. _____ the street by walking in the _______.
8. After you cross the street, _______ to your left.
9. __________ walking until you reach the ____________.
10. Finally, you are at the underpass.
11. Cross the street _______ the underpass.
12. When you get ______ of the underpass, you see the park in _________ of you.

13. Enjoy your afternoon at the park.

C

1. 아름다운 일요일 오후이고 당신은 산책을 하고 싶습니다.
2. 당신은 근처 공원에 가고 싶습니다.
3. 집을 나서서 인도로 걸어가세요.
4. 저기 신호등이 있습니다.
5. 신호등에서 멈추세요.
6. 신호등이 빨간불에서 파란불로 바뀔 때까지 기다리세요.
7. 파란불이 왔습니다. 건널목으로 갈을 건너세요.
8. 길을 건넌 후 왼쪽으로 도세요.
9. 지하도가 나올 때까지 계속 걸어가세요.
10. 마침내 지하도에 왔습니다.
11. 지하도로 길을 건너세요.
12. 지하도를 빠져나오면 당신 앞에 공원이 보입니다.
13. 공원에서 오후를 즐기세요.

39 Dressing for Winter

A

1. It's freezing today. You'd better wear heavy clothes.
2. Wear a long-sleeved shirt.
3. Wear a wool sweater, long pants, and thick wool socks.
4. Before going outdoors, put on a heavy coat.
5. Don't forget gloves or mittens.
6. Wrap a scarf around your neck.
7. Put on earmuffs.
8. Put on a hat and long boots.
9. That's enough to keep you warm.
10. Ready? Go out.

Key Vocabulary

- freezing: 영하의, 몹시 추운
- had('d) better ~: ~하는 게 낫다
- heavy clothes: 두꺼운 옷
- wear: 입다 (주로 상태를 나타낼 때 쓴다.)
- long-sleeved: 긴 팔의 (cf. short-sleeved: 짧은 팔의)
- go outdoors: 밖으로 나가다
- put on: 입다 (주로 동작을 나타낼 때 쓴다.)
- gloves: 손가락이 있는 장갑
- mittens: 벙어리장갑
- wrap A around B: A를 B주위로 두르다
- That's enough: 그 정도면 충분하다.
- to keep you warm: 당신을 따뜻하게 유지하기 위하여
- Ready? = Are you ready?: 준비됐나요?

B

1. It's _________ today. You'd better wear _______ clothes.
2. Wear a _______________shirt.
3. Wear a wool sweater, long pants, and _____ wool socks.
4. Before going outdoors, _______ on a heavy coat.
5. Don't forget gloves or ___________.
6. Wrap a scarf __________ your neck.
7. Put on ____________.
8. ________ on a hat and long boots.
9. That's _________ to keep you warm.
10. Ready? Go out.

C

1. 오늘은 몹시 춥습니다. 옷을 두껍게 입는 게 좋습니다.
2. 긴 팔 셔츠를 입으세요.
3. 울 스웨터와 긴 바지를 입고, 두꺼운 울 양말을 신으세요.
4. 바깥으로 나가기 전, 두터운 코트를 입으세요.
5. 장갑(또는 벙어리장갑)을 잊지 마세요.
6. 스카프를 목 주위에 두르세요.
7. 귀마개를 하세요.
8. 모자를 쓰고 긴 부츠를 신으세요.
9. 그 정도면 몸을 따뜻하게 보존하는 데 충분합니다.
10. 준비됐나요? 나가세요.

40 A Haircut

A

1. Your hair is getting long. You need a haircut.
2. Go to the beauty shop.
3. The hairdresser is busy.
4. Have a seat and wait your turn.
5. Read a magazine while you wait."Next!"
6. It's your turn. Get up.
7. Go sit in the hairdresser's chair.
8. Chat with the hairdresser.

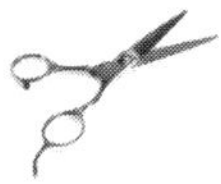

9. Watch him/her in the mirror while he/she works.
10. O.K. All done. Look at yourself in the mirror.
11. You look great! Get up and pay the hairdresser.
12. What a terrific hairdresser! Give him/her a tip.

Key Vocabulary

- It is getting long: 길어지고 있다.
- haircut: 이발, 머리 자르기
- beauty shop: 미용실
- hairdresser: 미용사
- Have a seat.: 앉다.
- wait: 기다리다
- turn: 차례, 순서
- while ~: ~하는 동안
- get up: 일어서다
- go sit: 가서 앉다
- chat: 잡담하다
- All done: 완성되다.
- look at ~: ~을 보다
- look great: 근사해 보이다
- pay: 값을 지불하다
- terrific: 대단한, 훌륭한
- What a terrific hairdresser!: 대단한 미용사이구나!

B

1. Your hair is getting long. You need a __________.
2. Go to the _________ shop.
3. The __________ is busy.
4. Have a seat and wait your ________.
5. Read a magazine ________ you wait. "Next!"
6. It's your ________. Get up.
7. Go ____ in the hairdresser's chair.
8. ________ with the hairdresser.
9. Watch him/her in the mirror while he/she ________.
10. O.K. All ________. Look at __________ in the mirror.
11. You look great! Get up and _______ the hairdresser.
12. What a ___________ hairdresser! Give him/her a tip.

C

1. 당신의 머리가 길어지고 있습니다. 당신은 이발이 필요합니다.
2. 미용실로 가세요.
3. 미용사가 바쁩니다.
4. 앉아서 당신의 차례를 기다리세요.
5. 기다리는 동안 잡지를 읽으세요. "다음!"
6. 당신 차례입니다. 일어서세요.
7. 미용사의 의자에 가서 앉으세요.
8. 미용사와 잡담하세요.
9. 그/그녀가 일하는 동안 거울 속의 그/그녀를 보세요.
10. 오케이. 다 됐습니다. 거울 속의 자신을 보세요.
11. 당신은 근사해 보입니다. 일어나서 미용사에게 요금을 주세요.
12. 대단한 미용사이군요! 그/그녀에게 팁을 주세요.

41 Taking Pictures

A

1. You're going to take some pictures of your friends.
2. Load your camera and wind it.
3. Now, you are ready.
4. Tell your friends where to stand.
5. Look through the camera.
6. Tell them to stand closer together.
7. Oh, it's too close.
8. Tell them to spread out.
9. Fine. It's just right.
10. Tell everybody to smile and press the button.
11. Tell them all to stay where they are.
12. Take another picture.

Key Vocabulary

- take a picture: 사진을 찍다
- load the camera: 사진기에 필름을 장착하다
- wind: 감다
- where to stand: 어디에 서야 하는지, 서야 할 장소
- look through ~ : ~ 를 통해서 보다
- stand closer together: 서로 더 가까이 서다
- too close: 너무 가까운
- spread out: 펼치다, 떨어지다
- It's just right.: 딱 됐다, 좋다.
- where they are: 그들이 있는 곳에
- another: 또 하나

B

1. You're going to ________ some pictures of your friends.
2. _________ your camera and _________ it.
3. Now, you are __________.
4. Tell your friends where ______ stand.
5. Look __________ the camera.
6. Tell them to stand __________ together.
7. Oh, it's ________ close.
8. Tell them to ___________ out.
9. Fine. It's ________ right.
10. Tell everybody ______ smile and press the button.
11. Tell them all to stay __________ they are.
12. Take ___________ picture.

C

1. 당신은 친구들의 사진을 몇 장 찍으려고 합니다.
2. 카메라에 필름을 넣고 감으세요.
3. 자, 준비가 되었습니다.
4. 친구들에게 어디에 서야 하는지 얘기하세요.
5. 카메라를 통해서 보세요.
6. 그들에게 좀더 가까이 서라고 얘기하세요.
7. 아, 너무 가깝습니다.
8. 조금 떨어지라고 얘기하세요.
9. 좋습니다. 딱 됐습니다.
10. 모두 웃으라고 얘기하고 버튼을 누르세요.
11. 모두 그 자리에 있으라고 말하세요.
12. 한 장 더 찍으세요.

42 Watching TV

A

1. Go to the refrigerator in the kitchen.
2. Open the freezer.
3. Get the ice cream out.
4. Close the freezer and the refrigerator.
5. Put some ice cream in a bowl.
6. Leave the carton on the counter.
7. Go into your room.
8. Turn on the T.V.

9. Sit down and watch your favorite program.
10. Eat your ice cream. Umm··· Delicious!
11. You ate it up and go back for more.
12. Oh no! The ice cream's melted!

Key Vocabulary

- refrigerator: 냉장고
- freezer: 냉동고, 냉동실
- get ~ out: ~을 끄집어내다
- put A in B: A를 B에 담다
- bowl: 그릇
- leave: 남겨두다
- carton: (판지로 만들어진) 통
- turn on: 켜다
- favorite: 가장 좋아하는
- eat up: 다 먹어버리다
- go back: 돌아가다
- The ice cream's melted: 아이스크림이 다 녹아버렸다

B

1. Go to the ______________ in the kitchen.
2. Open the __________.
3. Get the ice cream ______.
4. _______ the freezer and the refrigerator.
5. Put some ice cream in a _______.
6. __________ the carton on the counter.
7. Go into your room.
8. ______ on the T.V.
9. Sit down and watch your _________ program.
10. Eat your ice cream. Umm … ____________!
11. You ate it ______ and go back for _______.
12. Oh no! The ice cream's __________!

C

1. 부엌에 있는 냉장고로 가세요.
2. 냉동실을 여세요.
3. 아이스크림을 끄집어내세요.
4. 냉동실과 냉장고 문을 닫으세요.
5. 아이스크림을 그릇에 담으세요.
6. 아이스크림 통을 카운터에 남겨두세요.
7. 당신 방으로 들어가세요.
8. TV를 켜세요.
9. 앉아서 당신이 가장 좋아하는 프로그램을 보세요.
10. 아이스크림을 먹으세요. 음… 맛있다!
11. 다 먹어버렸어요. 좀더 가지러 가세요.
12. 아이고! 아이스크림이 녹아버렸네요!

43 Gardening

A

1. Turn the soil with a spade.
2. Plant some seeds.
3. Cover them with a mound of soil.
4. Plant some seedlings.
5. Tie them to small stakes.
6. Water the garden.
7. Weed the garden.
8. Prune extra leaves from some plants.
9. Check for harmful insects.
10. Spray insecticide on some plants.
11. Put some fertilizer on the soil.
12. Finally, pick some flowers for the house.

Key Vocabulary

- turn: 뒤엎다
- spade: 삽
- seed: 씨앗
- a mound of soil: 흙 둔덕
- tie A to B: A를 B에 묶다
- water: 물을 뿌리다
- prune: 떼어내다, 잘라내다
- harmful insect: 해로운 곤충
- put A on B: A를 B에 뿌리다
- pick flowers: 꽃을 꺾다
- soil: 흙, 토양
- plant: 심다
- cover A with B: A를 B로 덮다
- seedling: 묘목
- stake: 막대기
- weed: 잡초를 뽑다
- extra leaves: 여분의 잎들, 필요 없는 잎들
- insecticide: 해충제
- fertilizer: 비료

B

1. Turn the ________ with a spade.
2. Plant some __________.
3. Cover them with a ________ of soil.
4. Plant some _________.
5. Tie them to small ___________.
6. ________ the garden.
7. ________ the garden.
8. _________ extra leaves from some plants.
9. Check for _________ insects.
10. Spray ____________ on some plants.
11. Put some ____________ on the soil.
12. Finally, ________ some flowers for the house.

C

1. 삽으로 흙을 뒤집으세요.
2. 씨를 좀 심으세요.
3. 그것들을 흙으로 도톰하게 덮으세요.
4. 묘목을 좀 심으세요.
5. 그것들을 작은 막대기에 묶으세요.
6. 정원에 물을 뿌리세요.
7. 정원의 잡초를 뽑으세요.
8. 몇몇 나무에서 필요 없는 잎들을 떼어내세요.
9. 해로운 곤충들이 있는지 살펴보세요.
10. 몇몇 나무들에는 해충제를 뿌리세요.
11. 흙에 비료를 좀 뿌리세요.
12. 마지막으로, 집을 위해서 꽃을 좀 꺾으세요.

44 Going to a Movie

A

1. Go to the movie theater with your friend.
2. Buy two tickets at the ticket window.
3. Give them to the ticket taker at the door.
4. Go into the lobby.
5. Buy some popcorn and something to drink.
6. Go into the theater.
7. Look for the seat numbers.
8. There they are! Go and sit down.
9. Watch the movie enjoying the pop corn and drink.
10. Some part of the movie is sad, some part is scary and some part is funny.
11. You cry, scream and laugh.
12. Finally, the movie is over.
    How did you like it?

Key Vocabulary

- ticket window: 매표소
- ticket taker: 표 받는 사람
- something to drink: 마실 것
- go into ~: ~로 들어가다
- look for ~: ~을 찾다
- There they are!: 저기 있네요!
- scary: 무서운, 소름끼치는
- funny: 재미있는 우스운
- scream: 소리 지르다
- The movie is over.: 영화가 끝나다.
- How did you like it?: 어땠어요?

B

1. Go to the movie theater _______ your friend.
2. Buy two tickets at the ticket ___________.
3. Give them to the ticket __________ at the door.
4. Go _______ the lobby.
5. Buy some popcorn and something _____ drink.
6. Go into the theater.
7. Look _______ the seat numbers.
8. ___________ they are! Go and sit down.
9. Watch the movie _________ the pop corn and drink.
10. Some part of the movie is sad, some part is _______ and some part is funny.
11. You cry, _________ and laugh.
12. Finally, the movie is ________. ________ did you like it?

C

1. 친구랑 영화관으로 가세요.
2. 매표소에서 표를 2장 사세요.
3. 문에서 표 받는 사람에게 표를 주세요.
4. 로비로 들어가세요.
5. 팝콘과 마실 것을 좀 사세요.
6. 상영관으로 들어가세요.
7. 좌석을 찾으세요.
8. 저기 있네요. 가서 앉으세요.
9. 팝콘과 음료를 즐기면서 영화를 보세요.
10. 어떤 부분은 슬프고, 어떤 부분은 무섭고, 어떤 부분은 웃기네요.
11. 당신은 울고, 소리 지르고, 웃습니다.
12. 마침내 영화가 끝났습니다. 어땠어요?

45 Painting a Picture

A

1. You're going to paint a picture.
2. Spread out some old newspapers.
3. Take out a piece of paper.
4. Open the color palette.
5. Pick up the paintbrush.
6. Paint a rainbow.
7. Let it dry.
8. Close the palette and put it away.
9. Wash the paint out of the brush.
10. Wipe it dry with tissue paper.
11. Hang the painting on the wall.
12. Fold up the newspapers and put them away.

Key Vocabulary

- paint a picture: 그림을 그리다
- spread out: 펼치다
- take out: 끄집어내다
- a piece of paper: 종이 한 장
- pick up: 집어 들다
- paintbrush: 그림 그리는 붓, 화필
- let: (~하게)하다, 두다
- palette: (화가의) 팔레트
- put away: (물건을) 치우다
- wash A out of B: B에서 A를 씻어내다
- wipe it dry: 닦아서 물기를 없애다
- tissue paper: 휴지, 화장지
- hang: 걸다, 매달다
- fold up: 접다

B

1. You're going to ________ a picture.
2. __________ out some old newspapers.
3. Take out a ________ of paper.
4. _________ the color palette.
5. _________ up the paintbrush.
6. Paint a __________.
7. ________ it dry.
8. Close the palette and put it ________.
9. ________ the paint out of the brush.
10. ________ it dry with tissue paper.
11. _______ the painting on the wall.
12. _______ up the newspapers and put them _______.

C

1. 당신은 그림을 그리려 합니다.
2. 오래된 신문지 몇 장을 펴세요.
3. 종이 한 장을 끄집어내세요.
4. 컬러 팔레트를 여세요.
5. 그림붓을 집어 드세요.
6. 무지개를 그리세요.
7. 마르도록 두세요.
8. 팔레트를 닫고 치우세요.
9. 붓의 페인트를 물로 씻어내세요.
10. 화장지로 닦아서 물기를 없애세요.
11. 그림을 벽에 거세요.
12. 신문을 접어서 치우세요.

46 A Beautiful Day

A

1. What a beautiful sunny day!
2. Sigh and go outside.
3. Stretch and yawn.
4. Lie down in the sun.
5. Oh, it's too hot!
6. You're sweating.
7. Sit up and look for a shady place.
8. Ah! There's a big shady tree.
9. Walk over to it.
10. Sit down in the shade.
11. Oh, it's nice and cool here.
12. Sigh, stretch and yawn again.
13. Lie down in the shade and go to sleep.

Key Vocabulary

- What a beautiful day!: 아, 아름다운 날씨구나!
- sigh: 한숨을 쉬다
- go outside: 밖으로 나가다
- stretch: 기지개를 켜다
- yawn: 하품하다
- lie down in the sun: 양지에 눕다
- sweat: 땀, 땀 흘리다
- sit up: 일어나 앉다
- look for: 찾다
- shady: 그늘진
- walk over to ~: ~로 걸어가다
- cool: 서늘한
- lie down: 눕다
- go to sleep: 잠들다

B

1. What a beautiful ________ day!
2. ________ and go outside.
3. Stretch and ________.
4. ________ down in the sun.
5. Oh, it's too _______!

6. You're ____________.
7. Sit up and look for a ___________ place.
8. Ah! There's a big __________ tree.
9. Walk _________ to it.
10. Sit down in the ___________.
11. Oh, it's nice and ________ here.
12. Sigh, __________ and yawn again.
13. Lie ________ in the shade and go ______ sleep.

C

1. 아, 정말 아름다운 화창한 날이구나!
2. 한숨을 쉬고 밖으로 나가세요.
3. 기지개를 켜고 하품을 하세요.
4. 양지에 누우세요.
5. 아, 너무 뜨겁습니다!
6. 당신은 땀을 흘리고 있네요.
7. 일어나 앉아서 그늘진 곳을 찾으세요.
8. 아! 저기 그늘이 있는 큰 나무가 있네요.
9. 그리로 걸어가세요.
10. 그늘에 앉으세요.
11. 아, 이곳은 근사하고 시원하네요.
12. 다시 한숨을 쉬고 기지개를 켜고 하품을 하세요.
13. 그늘에 누워서 잠이 듭니다.

47 A Rainy Day

A

1. It's raining outside.
2. But you want to go out for a movie.

3. Spread your umbrella.
4. Walk in the rain to the theater.
5. There's a big puddle on the way.

6. Stay away from it. Don't step over it.
7. Suddenly, it starts pouring and the wind gets high, too.

8. Your umbrella doesn't work.
9. Look at you! You're all wet!
10. Fold your umbrella and run to the theater.
11. Finally, you've arrived at the theater.
12. Take out your handkerchief.
13. Dry yourself before you go in to watch the movie.

Key Vocabulary

- go out for ~: ~를 위해 나가다
- puddle: 물웅덩이
- step over: 밟다
- It start pouring: (비가) 퍼붓기 시작하다.
- The umbrella doesn't work: 우산이 소용없다.
- take out: 끄집어내다
- spread umbrella: 우산을 펴다
- on the way: 가는 길에, 도중에
- stay away from ~: ~를 피하다, ~로부터 떨어지다
- The wind gets high: 바람이 거세지다.
- look at ~: ~을 보다
- fold the umbrella: 우산을 접다
- dry: 말리다, 건조시키다

B

1. It's raining ________.

2. But you want to go out _____ a movie.
3. _________ your umbrella.
4. Walk in the rain ___ the theater.

5. There's a big _________ on the way.
6. Stay _______ from it. Don't step over it.
7. ___________, it starts ________ and the wind gets high, too.

8. Your umbrella doesn't ________.
9. Look at you! You're all ______!
10. _______ your umbrella and run to the theater.
11. Finally, you've _________ at the theater now.
12. ________ out your handkerchief.
13. _______ yourself before you go in to watch the movie.

C

1. 밖에 비가 옵니다.
2. 하지만 당신은 영화를 보러 나가고 싶습니다.
3. 우산을 펴세요.
4. 빗속을 걸어서 영화관으로 가세요.
5. 가는 길에 큰 물웅덩이가 있습니다.
6. 근처에 가지 마세요. 밟지 마세요.
7. 갑자기 비가 퍼붓기 시작하고 바람도 거세어집니다.
8. 우산이 소용없네요.
9. 당신을 보세요! 다 젖었네요!
10. 우산을 접고 극장으로 뛰어가세요.
11. 마침내, 당신은 극장에 도달하였습니다.
12. 손수건을 꺼내세요.
13. 영화 보러 안으로 들어가기 전에 몸을 말리세요.

48 Playing a CD

A

1. You love music and have a huge collection of CDs.
2. You are free now and want to listen to the music.
3. Choose a CD case from the shelf and take the CD out of the case.
4. Hold the disc at the edge.
5. Load the disc into the tray of the CD player.

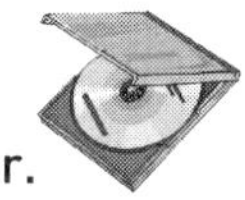

6. Pick up the remote controller.
7. Punch in the number of the track you want to listen to.
8. Enjoy the music.
9. Finally, the music is over.

10. Eject the CD with the remote controller.
11. Put the CD back in the case.

12. Put the case back on the shelf.

Key Vocabulary

- huge: 방대한, 많은 양의
- free: 한가한, 시간적 여유가 있는
- edge: 가장자리
- load A into B: A를 B에 장착하다
- remote controller: 리모컨
- track: 트랙, 궤도
- be over: 끝나다
- collection: 수집, 모음
- shelf: 선반
- take A out of B: A를 B에서 끄집어내다
- tray: 쟁반, 접시
- punch in: 입력하다
- finally: 마침내
- eject: 나가게 하다, 빼내다
- put A back in B: B안에 도로 넣다
- put A back on B: B 위에 도로 놓다

B

1. You love music and have a huge __________ of CDs.
2. You are ______ now and want to listen to the music.
3. Choose a CD case from the ________ and _______ the CD out of the case.

4. Hold the disc at the ________.
5. _______ the disc into the tray of the CD player.
6. _______ up the remote controller.
7. _________ in the number of the track you want to listen to.

8. Enjoy the music.
9. Finally, the music is ________.
10. _________ the CD with the remote controller.

11. Put the CD _________ in the case.
12. Put the case back _____ the shelf.

C

1. 당신은 음악을 좋아해서 CD를 많이 소장하고 있습니다.
2. 당신은 지금 한가해서 음악을 듣고 싶습니다.
3. 선반에서 CD 케이스를 하나 선택해서 CD를 케이스에서 꺼내세요.
4. 디스크 가장자리를 잡으세요.
5. 디스크를 CD 플레이어의 CD 넣는 곳에 장착하세요.
6. 리모컨을 집어 드세요.
7. 당신이 듣고 싶은 트랙의 번호를 입력하세요.
8. 음악을 즐기세요.
9. 마침내, 음악이 끝났습니다.
10. 리모컨을 이용해서 CD를 빼내세요.
11. CD를 케이스에 도로 넣으세요.
12. 케이스를 선반 위에 도로 놓으세요.

49 Reading a Magazine

A

1. You are free now and want to read a magazine.
2. Pick up the latest issue of your favorite magazine.
3. Wow, it includes so many ads and it's heavy.
4. Look at some of the ads and flip through the magazine.
5. Oh, here's an interesting article.
6. Read the article, looking at the pictures.
7. Finally, you finished reading the article.
8. Look for another one. Oh, here's one!
9. It's on what you are very concerned with.
10. Read it carefully.
11. Finally, you finished reading the article.
12. Put the magazine away and get some rest.

Key Vocabulary

- free: 한가한
- latest issue: 가장 최근 호
- magazine: 잡지
- favorite: 애호하는
- include: 포함하다
- ad(advertisement): 광고
- flip through: (책장을) 쭉 넘기다
- article: 기사, 논문
- finally: 마침내
- look for: 찾다
- another one: 또 하나
- on ~: ~에 관한
- be concerned with ~: ~에 관심을 갖다, 관여하다
- carefully: 조심스레, 유심히
- put away: 치우다
- get some rest: 휴식을 취하다

B

1. You are ________ now and want to read a magazine.
2. Pick up the __________ issue of your favorite magazine.
3. Wow, it includes so many _______ and it's heavy.
4. Look at some of the ads and _____ through the magazine.
5. Oh, here's an interesting ___________.
6. Read the article, looking _____ the pictures.
7. Finally, you ___________ reading the article.

8. Look ______ another one. Oh, here's one!
9. It's on what you are very ______________ with.
10. Read it ___________.
11. __________, you finished reading the article.
12. Put the magazine _______ and get some ________.

C

1. 당신은 지금 한가해서 잡지를 읽으려 합니다.
2. 당신이 가장 좋아하는 잡지의 최근호를 집으세요.
3. 아이고, 광고를 많이 포함하고 있어서 무겁습니다.
4. 몇몇 광고들을 보고 잡지 페이지를 쭉 넘기세요.
5. 아, 여기 재미있는 기사가 있네요.
6. 그림을 보면서 기사를 읽으세요.
7. 마침내 당신은 기사를 다 읽었습니다.
8. 또 다른 기사를 찾아보세요. 아, 여기 하나 있네요.
9. 당신이 관심을 갖고 있는 것에 대한 것입니다.
10. 유심히 읽으세요.
11. 마침내 당신은 그 기사를 다 읽었습니다.
12. 잡지를 치우고 휴식을 취하세요.

50 Watching a Video

A

1. You want to watch a movie on the VCR.
2. Go to the video shop and rent a video tape.
3. Come back home with the video tape.
4. Sit in front of the TV and take the tape out of the case.

5. With the remote controller, switch the TV to the video setting and turn the VCR on.

6. Load the video tape into it and start it.
7. The movie is on. Watch the movie.
8. Ah, you like this part.
9. Rewind the tape and watch it again.

10. Finally, the movie is over.
11. Stop the tape, rewind and eject it.
12. Take the video to the shop and return it.

Key Vocabulary

- VCR (Video Cassette Recorder): 비디오 상영 기계
- rent: 대여하다, 빌리다
- in front of ~: ~앞에
- take A out of B: A를 B에서 꺼내다
- remote controller: 리모콘
- switch A to B: A를 B로 바꾸다, 전환하다
- turn on: 켜다
- on: 상영 중인
- rewind: 다시 감다
- over: 끝난
- eject: 빼내다
- take a to B: A를 B로 가져가다
- return: 돌려주다

B

1. You want to watch a movie _____ the video.
2. Go to the video shop and _______ the video tape.
3. Come ________ home with the video tape.
4. Sit in ________ of the TV and take the tape _______ of the case.

5. With the _________ controller, switch the TV to the video setting and turn the VCR _____.

6. Load the video tape _______ it and start it.
7. The movie is ______. Watch the movie.

8. Ah, this part is great!
9. _________ the tape and watch it again.
10. Finally, the movie is _________.
11. Stop the tape, rewind and _________ it.
12. Take the video to the shop and __________ it.

C

1. 당신은 비디오로 영화를 보고 싶어합니다.
2. 비디오 가게로 가서 비디오 테잎을 빌리세요.
3. 비디오 테잎을 가지고 집으로 돌아오세요.
4. TV 앞에 앉아서 케이스에서 테잎을 꺼내세요.
5. 리모콘으로 TV를 비디오 세팅으로 바꾸고 VCR을 트세요.
6. 비디오 테잎을 넣고 시작하세요.
7. 영화가 나옵니다. 영화를 보세요.
8. 아, 이 부분이 근사합니다.
9. 테잎을 다시 감아서 그 부분을 다시 보세요.
10. 마침내 영화가 끝납니다.
11. 테잎을 멈추고, 다시 감아서 끄집어내세요.
12. 비디오를 가게로 가져가서 돌려주세요.

SECTION 4

Food & Drink

51 Chewing Gum

A

1. Go to a store and buy a pack of chewing gum.
2. Open the pack and take out a piece.
3. Unwrap it and put it in your mouth.
4. Chew it but don't make noise with it.
5. The noise you make can disturb other people.
6. Don't throw away the wrapper. You will need it later.
7. Keep the pack of gum in your purse.
8. Keep chewing.
9. Do you want to stop chewing?
10. Take out the gum from your mouth.
11. Wrap it in the wrapper.
12. Throw the wrapper into the garbage can.

Key Vocabulary

- a pack of chewing gum~: 껌 한 통
- piece: 조각, 낱개
- unwrap: 포장을 풀다
- make noise: 소음을 내다
- disturb: 방해하다
- throw away: 던져버리다
- wrapper: 포장지
- later: 나중에
- purse: 지갑, 핸드백
- keep ~ing: 계속해서 ~하다
- stop ~ing: ~하기를 멈추다
- take out A from B: A를 B에서 꺼내다
- throw A into B: A를 B 속으로 던져버리다
- garbage can: 쓰레기통

B

1. Go to a store and buy a ________ of chewing gum.
2. Open the pack and take out a _________.
3. _____________it and put it in your mouth.
4. Chew it but don't _________ noise with it.
5. The noise you make can ___________ other people.
6. Don't throw away the ________. You will need it later.
7. ________ the pack of gum in your purse.

8. Keep __________.
9. Do you want to ________ chewing?
10. Take _____ the gum from your mouth.
11. _________ it in the wrapper.
12. _________ the wrapper into the garbage can.

C

1. 상점으로 가서 껌 한 통을 사세요.
2. 통을 열어서 껌 한 개를 꺼내세요.
3. 껌 포장지를 풀어서 껌을 입에 넣으세요.
4. 껌을 씹으세요. 하지만 소음은 내지 마세요.
5. 당신이 내는 소음이 다른 사람들을 방해할 수 있습니다.
6. 포장지는 버리지 마세요. 나중에 필요할 겁니다.
7. 껌 통을 가방 속에 보관하세요.
8. 계속 씹으세요.
9. 그만 씹고 싶습니까?
10. 입에서 껌을 빼내세요.
11. 포장지에 그것을 싸세요.
12. 포장지를 쓰레기통에 던져버리세요.

52 Scrambled Eggs

A

1. You're going to fix scrambled eggs for your family.
2. Break four eggs and drop them into a bowl.
3. Pick up the egg beater and beat the eggs.
4. Add some salt and a little milk.
5. Mix them with a spoon.
6. Oil the pan and put it on the stove.
7. Turn on the stove and heat it up.
8. Pour the egg mixture into the pan.
9. Cook it by keeping stirring it.
10. Now, you can see it's almost dry.
11. Turn off the heat.
12. Put it on a plate and let your family enjoy it.

Key Vocabulary

- fix: 요리를 하다, 만들다 (=make)
- drop A into B: A를 B에 떨어뜨리다
- egg beater: 달걀 젓개
- beat the egg: 달걀을 젓다
- add: 첨가하다, 보태다
- oil the pan: (프라이)팬에 기름을 두르다
- turn on the stove: 스토브를 켜다
- heat up: 열을 가해 데우다
- pour A into B: A를 B에 붓다
- keep stirring: 계속 젓다
- dry: 마른, 물기가 없는
- turn off the heat: 불을 끄다
- let: (~로 하여금) ~하게 하다

B

1. You're going to ______ scrambled eggs for your family.
2. ________ some eggs and drop them into a bowl.
3. Pick up the egg beater and ________ the eggs.
4. _______ some salt and a little milk.
5. _______ them with a spoon.
6. _______ the pan and put it on the stove.
7. ________ on the stove and ________ it up.
8. ________ the egg mixture into the pan.
9. Cook it by keeping __________ it.
10. Now, you can see it's almost _______.
11. Turn ______ the heat.
12. Put it on a plate and _______ your family enjoy it.

C

1. 당신은 가족을 위하여 스크램블드에그를 만들려고 합니다.
2. 대접에다 달걀 몇 개를 깨 넣으세요.
3. 달걀 젓개를 집어서 달걀을 저으세요.
4. 소금 약간과 우유를 좀 넣으세요.
5. 그것들을 숟가락으로 섞으세요.
6. 프라이팬 기름을 두르고 스토브에 올리세요.
7. 스토브를 켜고 데우세요.
8. 달걀 섞은 것을 팬에 쏟아 부으세요.
9. 계속해서 저으면서 요리하세요.
10. 자, 당신은 그것의 물기가 거의 없어진 것을 볼 수 있습니다.
11. 불을 끄세요.
12. 그것을 접시에 담아 가족들이 즐기게 하세요.

53 Frying an Egg

A

1. You're going to fry an egg for lunch.
2. Turn on one of the burners on the stove.
3. Put the frying pan on the burner.
4. Put some butter in the pan and let it melt.
5. Crack an egg into the pan.
6. Great! The york is not broken.

7. Throw the shell into the garbage can.
8. The egg fries.
9. You'd like it well-done.

10. Flip it over once with a spatula.
11. It looks done.
12. Take it out of the pan and put it on a plate.

Key Vocabulary

- turn on: 켜다
- burner: 버너
- let: (~로 하여금) ~하게 하다
- melt: 녹다
- crack: 깨다 (=break)
- york: (달걀의) 노른자위 (cf. white: 흰자위)
- throw A into B: A를 B 속으로 던져버리다
- shell: 껍질
- garbage can: 쓰레기통
- well-done: 완전히 익힌
  (cf. rare: 덜 구워진, 덜 익은; sunny-side up: 한쪽만 익힌)
- flip over: 뒤집다
- spatula: 뒤집개
- It looks done: 다 된 것 같다.
- Take A out of B: A를 B에서 꺼내다

B

1. You're going to fry an egg for lunch.
2. Turn on one of the ________ on the stove.
3. Put the ________ pan on the burner.
4. Put some butter in the pan and let it ________.
5. ________ an egg into the pan.
6. Great! The ______ is not broken.

7. Throw the ______ into the garbage can.
8. The egg _______.

9. You'd like it ____________.
10. Flip it over once with a ___________.
11. It looks _________.
12. Take it ______ of the pan and put it on a plate.

C

1. 당신은 점심을 위해서 달걀을 하나 프라이하려고 합니다.
2. 스토브의 버너 중 하나를 켜세요.
3. 프라이팬을 버너 위에 올리세요.
4. 팬에 버터를 좀 넣고 녹이세요.
5. 팬에 달걀을 하나 깨어 넣으세요.
6. 훌륭합니다! 노른자위가 깨지지 않았어요.
7. 껍질은 쓰레기통에 던져버리세요.
8. 달걀이 프라이됩니다.
9. 당신은 그것이 완전히 익히고 싶습니다.
10. 뒤집개로 한 번 뒤집으세요.
11. 다 된 것 같습니다.
12. 팬에서 꺼내어 접시에 담으세요.

54 Making Toast

A

1. You want to eat a piece of toast.

2. Take out a slice of bread.
3. Put it in the toaster.
4. Push the starter down and wait a minute.
6. The toaster signals it's done!
7. Take out the toast and put it on the plate.
8. Spread some butter on it.
9. Watch it melt in.

10. Pour a spoonful of jam on the toast.
11. Spread it around with a knife.
12. Cut the toast in half.

13. Pick up one half and eat it.
14. It's good! Eat the other half, too.

Key Vocabulary

- a piece of toast: 토스트 한 조각
- a slice of bread: 자른 빵 한 조각
- starter: 시작 장치
- signal: 신호를 보내다
- spread A on B: A를 B 위에 펴 바르다, 흩뿌리다
- take out: 끄집어내다
- put A in B: A를 B에 넣다
- push down: 밑으로 밀다
- it's done: 다 됐다.
- melt in: 녹아서 스며들다
- pour: 붓다
- a spoonful of ~: ~ 한 숟가락
- spread around: 이리저리 펴 바르다
- cut in half: 반으로 자르다
- one half: 반 조각 하나
- pick up: 집어들다
- the other half: 나머지 반 조각

B

1. You want to eat a _________ of toast.
2. Take _____ a slice of bread.
3. Put it in the __________.
4. Push the starter ________ and ________ a minute.
5. The toaster __________ it's done!
6. ________ out the toast and put it on the plate.
7. __________ some butter on it.
8. Watch it _________ in.
9. Pour a _____________ of jam on the toast.
10. Spread it _________ with a knife.
11. Cut the toast in _________.
12. _________ up one half and eat it.
13. It's good! Eat the _________ half, too.

C

1. 당신은 토스트 한 조각을 먹고 싶습니다.
2. 얇게 썬 빵 한 조각을 꺼내세요.
3. 토스트기에 그것을 넣으세요.
4. 시작 장치를 밑으로 누르고 잠시 기다리세요.
5. 토스트기가 다 됐다는 신호를 보냅니다.
6. 토스트를 꺼내서 접시에 올려놓으세요.
7. 버터를 그 위에 펴 바르세요.
8. 버터가 녹아 스며드는 것을 보세요.
9. 한 스푼의 잼을 토스트 위에 부으세요.
10. 칼로 이리저리 펴 바르세요.
11. 토스트를 반으로 자르세요.
12. 반 조각을 집어들고 먹으세요.
13. 맛있어요! 나머지 반 조각을 먹으세요.

55 A Glass of Milk

A

1. You want to drink some milk.
2. Pour some milk into a glass.
3. Woops! Spill some of it on the table.
4. Go to the sink and pick up a rag.
5. Get it wet and wring it out.
6. Go back and wipe up the spilt milk.
7. Go back to the sink.
8. Rinse out the rag.
9. Hang it on the faucet.
10. Go back to the table where the milk is.
11. Drink your milk.
12. Be careful not to spill any more.

Key Vocabulary

- pour A into B: A를 B 속으로 따르다
- Whoops!: 어머나! 이런!
- spill: 쏟다
- pick up: 집어 들다, 집다
- rag: 행주
- get it wet: 적시다
- wring it out: 비틀어서 물기를 빼다
- wipe up: 닦아내다
- rinse out: 헹궈서 물기를 짜내다
- hang: 매달다, 널다
- faucet: 수도꼭지
- where ~ : ~인 곳에
- Be careful: 조심하다
- not ~ any more: 더 이상 ~않다

B

1. You want to drink some milk.
2. _________ some milk into a glass.
3. Woops! _________ some of it on the table.
4. Go to the sink and pick up a _________.
5. Get it wet and _________ it out.
6. Go back and ________ up the spilt milk.
7. Go ________ to the sink.
8. _________ out the rag.
9. Hang it on the ___________.

10. Go back to the table ________ the milk is.
11. Drink your milk.
12. Be careful not to spill any _________.

C

1. 당신은 우유를 좀 마시고 싶습니다.
2. 우유를 잔에다 좀 부으세요.
3. 아이고! 식탁 위에 그것을 좀 쏟았네요.
4. 싱크대로 가서 행주를 하나 집으세요.
5. 그것을 적셔서 짜세요.
6. 되돌아가서 쏟아진 우유를 닦으세요.
7. 싱크대로 도로 가세요.
8. 행주를 헹궈 물기를 제거하세요.
9. 수도꼭지 위에 그것을 걸어놓으세요.
10. 우유가 있는 식탁으로 도로 가세요.
11. 우유를 마시세요.
12. 더 이상 쏟지 않도록 조심하세요.

56 Breakfast Cereal

A

1. You're going to eat some cereal for breakfast.
2. Go get the cereal box and open it.
3. Pour some cereal into the bowl.
4. Oops! You spilt some of it on your table.
5. Pick it up and put it in the bowl.
6. Close the cereal box.
7. Sprinkle some sugar over the cereal.
8. Pour on some milk.
9. OK! it's done. Enjoy it with a spoon.
10. You're finished.
11. Take the empty bowl and spoon to the sink.
12. Wash them and put them in the dish drainer.

Key Vocabulary

- go get: 가서 가져오다
- pour A into B: A를 B 속으로 쏟아 붇다
- Oops!: 어머나, 이런!
- spill: 쏟다 (spilt: 쏟았다)
- pick up: 줍다
- put in: 넣다
- sprinkle: 흩어 뿌리다
- be finished: 마치다, 끝내다
- take A to B: A를 B로 가져가다
- dish drainer: 접시건조기

B

1. You're going to eat some cereal _____ breakfast.
2. Go get the cereal box and ________ it.
3. _________ some cereal into the bowl.
4. Oopes! you ________ some of it on your table.
5. Pick it ______ and put it in the bowl.
6. ________ the cereal box.
7. ___________ some sugar over the cereal.
8. __________ on some milk.
9. OK! it's done. Enjoy it with a spoon.
10. You're _____________.
11. ________ the empty bowl and spoon to the sink.
12. Wash them and put them in the dish __________.

C

1. 당신은 아침 식사로 시리얼을 먹을 겁니다.
2. 가서 시리얼 박스를 가져와서 여세요.
3. 시리얼을 대접에 좀 부으세요.
4. 아이고! 당신은 그것의 일부를 테이블 위에 쏟았습니다.
5. 주워서 대접에 담으세요.
6. 시리얼 박스를 닫으세요.
7. 시리얼 위에 설탕을 좀 뿌리세요.
8. 그 위에 우유를 부으세요.
9. 좋습니다. 다 됐습니다. 숟가락으로 그것을 즐기세요.
10. 다 먹었습니다.
11. 빈 대접과 숟가락을 싱크대로 가져가세요.
12. 그것들을 씻어서 접시건조기에 놓으세요.

57 Fixing Dinner

A

1. You are going to fix dinner for your family.
2. Measure the rice, wash it and cook it.
3. Take out a frozen fish from the freezer.

4. Put the fish in the microwave oven.
5. Set the timer and have it melt.

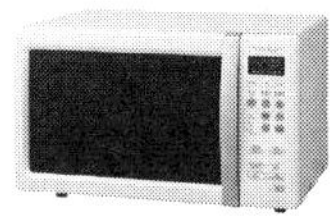

6. Take it out.
7. Run some water over it and rinse it.
8. Dry it with the kitchen towel.
9. Fry it in the frying pan.

10. It's done. Spread some salt over it.
11. The soup has boiled in the mean time.
12. Take out other side dishes from the refrigerator.
13. Set the table and enjoy your dinner.

Key Vocabulary

- fix dinner: 저녁을 만들다, 짓다. (=make dinner)
- measure: (양, 무게, 길이 등을) 재다
- frozen: 냉동된, 언
- take out: 끄집어내다
- dry: 건조시키다, 물기를 없애다
- It's done: 다 되었다.
- in the mean time: 그동안에
- side dish: 반찬
- set the table: 식탁을 차리다
- empty: 비어있는 빈
- have ~ melt: ~을 녹게 하다
- run water over ~: ~ 위로 물을 흘려보내다
- spread A over B: A를 B위로 흩뿌리다
- refrigerator: 냉장고
- pour on: 계속 붓다

B

1. You are going to ________ dinner for your family.
2. ____________ the rice, wash it and cook it.
3. Take out a __________ fish from the freezer.
4. _________ the fish in the microwave oven.
5. Set the timer and have it __________.

6. __________ it out.

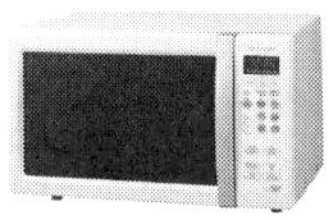

7. ________ some water over it and rinse it.
8. _______ it with the kitchen towel.
9. Fry it in the __________ pan.

10. It's done. _________ some salt over it.
11. The soup has __________ in the mean time.
12. Take out other ________ dishes from the refrigerator.
13. _________ the table and enjoy your dinner.

C

1. 당신은 가족을 위하여 저녁식사를 만들려고 합니다.
2. 쌀 양을 재고 씻어서 밥을 지으세요.
3. 냉동실에서 냉동된 생선을 한 마리 꺼내세요.
4. 생선을 전자레인지에 넣으세요.
5. 시간을 정해서 그것을 녹이세요.
6. 그것을 꺼내세요.
7. 그것 위로 물을 흘려보내서 헹구세요.
8. 키친 타올로 그것의 물기를 없애세요.
9. 프라이팬에서 그것을 프라이하세요.
10. 다 됐습니다. 위에 소금을 좀 뿌리세요.
11. 그동안에 국이 다 끓었네요.
12. 냉장고에서 다른 반찬들도 꺼내세요.
13. 식탁을 차리고 저녁식사를 즐기세요.

58 Making a Salad

A

1. You want to make a salad.
2. Get the material out of the refrigerator.
3. Rinse some lettuce by running water over it.
4. Drain it in a colander.
5. Rinse some tomatoes and cucumbers.
6. Slice them with a knife on a cutting board.
7. Mix the lettuce and the cucumber in a salad bowl.
8. Lay the tomato slices on top.
9. Sprinkle some grated cheese on the salad.
10. Pour some dressing on the salad.
11. Enjoy your salad.

Key Vocabulary

- get A out of B: A를 B에서 꺼내다 (=Take A out of B)
- material: 재료
- rinse: 물로 씻다, 헹구다
- lettuce: 상추
- drain: 물기를 빼다
- slice: 얇게 썰다
- cucumber: 오이
- lay: 놓다
- sprinkle: 뿌리다
- grated cheese: 강판으로 간 치즈
- refrigerator: 냉장고
- colander: 체
- run water over A: A 위로 물을 흘려보내다
- mix A and B: A와 B를 섞다
- cutting board: 도마
- on top: 제일 위에
- pour: 붓다

B

1. You want to make a salad.
2. Get the __________ out of the refrigerator.
3. __________ some lettuce by running water over it.
4. __________ it in a colander.
5. Rinse some tomatoes and __________.
6. ________ them with a knife on a _________ board.
7. _______ the lettuce and the cucumber in a salad bowl.
8. Lay the tomato slices on _______.
9. _________ some grated cheese on the salad.
10. Pour some __________ on the salad.
11. Enjoy your salad.

C

1. 당신은 샐러드를 만들고 싶습니다.
2. 냉장고에서 재료를 꺼내세요.
3. 흐르는 물에 상추를 좀 씻으세요.
4. 체로 상추 물기를 빼세요.
5. 토마토와 오이를 씻으세요.
6. 그것들을 도마 위에서 칼로 얇게 써세요.
7. 샐러드 그릇에다가 상추와 오이를 섞으세요.
8. 얇게 썬 토마토를 제일 위에 놓으세요.
9. 강판으로 간 치즈를 그 위에 좀 뿌리세요.
10. 샐러드 위에 드레싱을 좀 부으세요.
11. 샐러드를 즐기세요.

59 Making a Spaghetti

A

1. Dice an onion and fry it with some ground beef in a frying pan.
2. As the beef-and-onion mixture fries, stir it.
3. When the meat turns brown, turn off the burner.
4. Heat two cans of tomato sauce in a saucepan.
5. Add the mixture of beef and onions.
6. Stir it into the sauce with some spices.

7. Turn down the heat and let the sauce simmer.

8. Boil some water in another pan.
9. Put some spaghetti into the boiling water.

10. Boil it until it gets tender.
11. Drain the spaghetti in a colander.
12. Put the spaghetti on a plate and ladle some sauce over it.

Key Vocabulary

- dice: 깍두기 꼴로 썰다
- ground beef: 갈아 만든 쇠고기
- mixture: 섞은 것
- stir: 젓다
- turn brown: 갈색으로 변하다
- turn off: (불을) 끄다
- heat: 열을 가하다, 데우다
- add: 보태다, 첨가하다
- stir A into B: A를 B 속으로 저어 넣다
- turn down: 낮추다
- let ~: ~하게 하다
- simmer: 천천히 끓다
- get tender: 부드러워지다
- drain: 물기를 빼다
- colander: 체
- ladle A over B: 국자로 A를 B에 붓다
- spices: 양념, 향신료

B

1. ________ an onion and fry it with some _______ beef in a frying pan.
2. As the beef-and-onion ___________ fries, stir it.
3. When the meat ________ brown, turn off the burner.
4. _________ two cans of tomato sauce in a saucepan.
5. ________ the mixture of beef and onions.
6. Stir it into the sauce with some _________.

7. Turn _______ the heat and let the sauce _________.
8. ________ some water in another pan.

9. Put some spaghetti into the __________ water.
10. Boil it until it gets __________.
11. _________ the spaghetti in a colander.
12. Put the spaghetti on a plate and _____ some sauce over it.

C

1. 양파 하나를 깍두기 꼴로 자르고 간 쇠고기와 함께 프라이팬에 볶으세요.
2. 쇠고기와 양파를 섞은 것이 볶이는 동안 그것을 저으세요.
3. 고기가 갈색으로 변하면 버너를 끄세요.
4. 소스팬에 토마토소스 깡통 2개 분량을 데우세요.
5. 쇠고기와 양파 섞은 것을 첨가하세요.
6. 양념을 넣고 그것을 소스 속으로 저어 넣으세요.
7. 불을 낮추고 소스가 서서히 끓게 하세요.
8. 다른 팬에다가 물을 좀 끓이세요.
9. 스파게티를 끓는 물 속에 넣으세요.
10. 부드러워질 때까지 그것을 끓이세요.
11. 체로 스파게티의 물기를 빼세요.
12. 스파게티를 접시에 놓고 소스를 국자로 퍼서 부으세요.

60 Soup for Lunch

A

1. You're going to heat up some soup for lunch.
2. Open the can with the can opener.
3. Pour the soup into a pan and add one can of water.
4. Stir it up and put it on the stove.
5. Put on the lid and turn on the stove.
6. Wait for the soup to heat up.
7. Take off the lid and check it.
8. It's ready. Turn off the heat.
9. Pour some soup into your bowl.
10. It's still hot! Blow on it.
11. Wait for it to cool off.
12. O.K. Now take a sip. Umm! Perfect!

Key Vocabulary

- heat up: (열을 가해) 데우다 (=warm up)
- can opener: 깡통 따개
- pour A into B: A를 B 속으로 붓다
- add: 첨가하다, 보태다
- put on the lid: 뚜껑을 닫다
- take off the lid: 뚜껑을 열다
- Turn off the heat: 불을 끄다
- cool off: (열이) 식다
- perfect: 완벽한
- stir up: 휘젓다
- turn on the stove: 스토브를 켜다
- It's ready: 다 됐다, 준비되다.
- blow: (입으로) 불다
- take a sip: 한 모금 먹다, 마시다

B

1. You're going to ________ up some soup for lunch.
2. Open the can with the can _________.
3. Pour the soup into a pan and _______ one can of water.
4. _______ it up and put it on the stove.
5. Put on the ______ and turn on the stove.
6. ________ for the soup to heat up.
7. Take _____ the lid and check it.
8. It's ready. _________ off the heat.
9. _______ some soup into your bowl.
10. It's still hot! _______ on it.
11. Wait for it to ________ off.
12. Now take a ______. Umm! Perfect!

C

1. 당신은 점심을 위해서 스프를 좀 데우려고 합니다.
2. 깡통 따개로 깡통을 따세요.
3. 스프를 팬에다 붓고 물을 한 깡통 보태세요.
4. 그것을 저어서 스토브 위에 올리세요.
5. 뚜껑을 닫고 스토브를 켜세요.
6. 스프가 데워질 때까지 기다리세요.
7. 뚜껑을 열고 체크하세요.
8. 다 됐습니다. 불을 끄세요.
9. 접시에 스프를 좀 부으세요.
10. 아직 뜨겁습니다. 입으로 바람을 부세요.
11. 식을 때까지 기다리세요.
12. 이제 한 모금 먹어보세요. 음! 완벽하네요!

61 Preparing Vegetables

A

1. Get some carrots and broccoli.
2. Peel and slice the carrots.
3. Chop up some broccoli.
4. Throw the stalk away.
5. Rinse the broccoli.
6. Put some water in the saucepan.
7. Put the steamer basket inside.
8. Put the vegetables in the basket.
9. Put the lid on the saucepan.
10. Light the burner and wait.
11. The water boils and steams the vegetables.
12. It's done. Turn off the burner.
13. Take the vegetables out of the steam basket.

Key Vocabulary

- peel: 껍질을 벗기다
- slice: 얇게 썰다
- chop up: 잘게 썰다
- throw away: 버리다
- stalk: 줄기, 대
- rinse: 헹구다
- saucepan: 스튜냄비
- steamer basket: 찜 광주리
- inside: 안에
- vegetable: 야채
- put on: (뚜껑을) 닫다
- lid: 뚜껑
- light: 불을 붙이다
- boil: 끓다
- burner: 버너
- steam: 수증기를 가하다
- It's done.: 다 됐다.
- turn off: (불을) 끄다
- take A out of B: A를 B에서 꺼내다

B

1. Get some ________ and broccoli.
2. ________ and slice the carrots.
3. ________ up some broccoli.
4. Throw the stalk _________.
5. __________ the broccoli.
6. Put some water in the saucepan.
7. Put the steamer basket ___________.
8. Put the ______________ in the basket.
9. Put the ______ on the saucepan.
10. _________ the burner and wait.
11. The water _______ and steams the vegetables.
12. It's done. ________ off the burner.
13. Take the steamed vegetables ______.

C

1. 당근과 브로콜리를 좀 준비하세요.
2. 당근의 껍질을 벗기고 가늘게 써세요.
3. 브로콜리는 가늘게 써세요.
4. 줄기(대)는 버리세요.
5. 브로콜리를 헹구세요.
6. 스튜냄비에 물을 좀 넣으세요.
7. 찜 광주리를 안에 넣으세요.
8. 야채들을 광주리에 넣으세요.
9. 스튜냄비 뚜껑을 닫으세요.
10. 버너의 불을 켜고 기다리세요.
11. 물이 끓고 야채를 찝니다.
12. 다 됐습니다. 버너를 끄세요.
13. 쪄진 야채를 꺼내세요.

62 At a Restaurant

A

1. You're going out for dinner.
2. Walk into a restaurant. Wow! It's crowded.
3. Find a table that's not occupied.
4. Sit down.
5. Pick up the menu and look for something good.
6. The waitress/waiter comes.
7. Order what you want.
8. Unfold the napkin, put it on your lap, and wait.
9. Wow! It's a long wait. You're starving!
10. Finally, the food comes.
11. Take a sip of water.
12. Enjoy the meal.

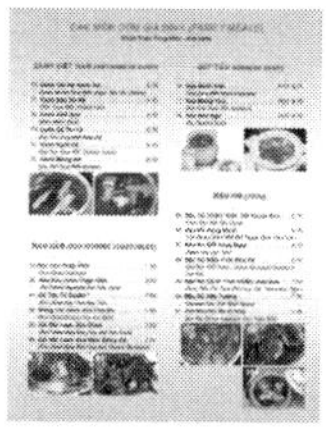

Key Vocabulary

- go our: 외출하다
- crowded: 복잡한, 붐비는
- occupied: 차지한, 점유된
- pick up: 집어 들다
- look for: 찾다
- something good: 좋은 것
- order: 주문하다
- unfold: 펴다 (cf. fold: 접다)
- lap: 무릎 (앉았을 때 허리부터 무릎까지의 부분) (cf. knee: 무릎 (관절), 무릎 마디)
- a long wait: 오랜 기다림
- starving: 배가 너무 고픈, 굶주리는
- finally: 마침내, 드디어
- a sip of water: 물 한 모금
- meal: 식사

B

1. You're going _____ for dinner.
2. Walk into a restaurant. Wow! It's _________.
3. Find a table that's not ___________.
4. Sit down.
5. ________ up the menu and look ____ something good.
6. The waitress/waiter comes.
7. ________ what you want.
8. _________ the napkin, put it on your _____, and wait.
9. Wow! It's a long ______.
   You're ___________!
10. _________, the food comes.
11. Take a _______ of water.
12. Enjoy the _________.

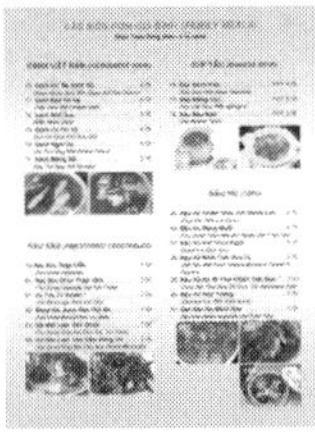

C

1. 당신은 저녁 외식을 하고자 합니다.
2. 레스토랑으로 걸어 들어가세요. 와! 복잡합니다.
3. 점유되지 않은 테이블을 하나 발견하세요.
4. 앉으세요.
5. 메뉴를 집어 들고 좋은 것을 찾아보세요.
6. 웨이트리스/웨이터가 옵니다.
7. 원하는 것을 주문하세요.
8. 냅킨을 펴서 무릎에 올려놓고 기다리세요.
9. 와! 오랜 기다림이네요. 당신은 배가 너무 고픕니다!
10. 마침내 음식이 나옵니다.
11. 물 한 모금 마시세요.
12. 식사를 즐기세요.

63 At a Fast Food Restaurant

A

1. You want to eat some fast food.
2. Go into a fast food restaurant.
3. Stand in the line and wait.
4. While waiting, read the menu and choose what you want.
5. Now, it's your turn.
   Whew... it was a long wait.
6. Order your food and drink, and pay the clerk.

7. Your food is ready.
8. The clerk puts the food and drink on your tray.
9. Take some paper napkins and a straw from the dispensers.
10. Find an empty table and enjoy your food.
11. When you're finished, throw the waste in the trash.

Key Vocabulary

- stand in the line: 줄 서다
- while ~: ~하는 동안
- choose: 선택하다
- turn: 차례, 순서
- a long wait: 오랜 기다림
- clerk: 점원
- ready: 준비된
- tray: (나르는) 쟁반
- paper napkin: 종이 냅킨
- straw: 빨대
- dispenser: (휴지, 종이컵 등을 내어주는) 용기, 장치
- empty table: 빈 테이블
- finish: 끝내다
- throw: 던져버리다
- waste: 쓰레기, 찌꺼기
- trash (can): 쓰레기(통)

B

1. You want to eat some fast food.
2. Go into a fast food ___________.
3. ________ in the line and wait.
4. _______ waiting, read the menu and choose _________ you want.
5. Now, it's your _______.
   Whew... it was a long ________.
6. Order your food and drink, and pay the _________.
7. Your food is _________.
8. The clerk puts the food and drink on your _______.
9. Take some paper napkins and a straw from the _______.
10. Find an _________ table and enjoy your food.
11. When you're finished, throw the ________ in the trash.

C

1. 당신은 패스트푸드를 먹고 싶습니다.
2. 패스트푸드점에 들어가세요.
3. 줄을 서서 기다리세요.
4. 기다리는 동안 메뉴를 읽고 원하는 것을 고르세요.
5. 자, 이제 당신 차례입니다. 휴~ 오랜 기다림이었네요.
6. 음식과 음료수를 주문하고 점원에게 값을 지불하세요.
7. 음식이 준비되었습니다.
8. 점원이 음식과 음료를 당신의 쟁반 위에 놓습니다.
9. 디스펜서에서 종이 냅킨과 빨대를 집으세요.
10. 빈 테이블을 찾아서 음식을 즐기세요.
11. 다 먹었으면 음식 찌꺼기는 쓰레기통에 버리세요.

64 Making Coffee

A

1. You're going to make coffee.
2. Plug in the coffee maker.
3. Scoop some ground coffee into the filter.
4. Put the filter into the coffee maker.
5. Pour some water into the coffee maker.
6. Turn on the coffee maker by pressing the switch.
7. The water heats up and drips through the ground coffee into the coffee pot.
8. The water stops dripping. It's done.
9. Go get a mug.
10. Pour the coffee into the mug.
11. Unplug the coffee maker.
12. Take the mug to the table and enjoy the coffee.

Key Vocabulary

- plug in: (전기) 플러그를 끼우다
- scoop A into B: A를 퍼내서 B에 담다
- ground coffee: 간 커피
- filter: (커피메이커의) 필터
- turn on: 켜다
- press: 누르다
- heat up: 데워지다
- drip through A into B: A를 통해 B로 (물이) 떨어지다
- It's done: 다 되었다.
- mug: 머그잔
- pour A into B: A를 B에 붓다
- unplug: 전기 플러그를 뽑다, 빼다

B

1. You're going to ________ coffee.
2. _______ in the coffee maker.
3. Scoop some _________ coffee into the filter.
4. _______ the filter into the coffee maker.
5. _________ some water into the coffee maker.
6. Turn on the coffee maker by _________ the switch.
7. The water ________ up and ________ through the ground coffee into the coffee pot.
8. The water stops _________. It's _______.
9. Go _______ a mug.
10. ________ the coffee into the mug.
11. __________ the coffee maker.
12. ________ the mug to the table and enjoy the coffee.

C

1. 당신은 커피를 만들려고 합니다.
2. 커피메이커 플러그를 꽂으세요.
3. 간 커피를 좀 퍼서 필터에 넣으세요.
4. 필터를 커피메이커에 넣으세요.
5. 커피메이커에 물을 좀 부으세요.
6. 스위치를 눌러서 커피메이커를 켜세요.
7. 물이 데워지면 간 커피를 통과해 커피메이커 용기로 떨어집니다.
8. 물 떨어지는 게 멈춥니다. 다 됐습니다.
9. 가서 머그잔을 하나 갖고 오세요.
10. 커피를 잔에다 부으세요.
11. 커피메이커 플러그를 빼세요.
12. 잔을 테이블로 가져가서 커피를 즐기세요.

SECTION 5

Shopping & Money

65 Shopping for a Coat

A

1. Winter is near at hand.
2. You need to get a new coat.
3. Look in the store windows.
4. Oh, there's a nice coat! Go inside.
5. Take a coat off the rack.
6. Take it off the hanger and try it on.
7. Look at yourself in the mirror.
8. Oh, it's too big. It's not your size.
9. Take it off.
10. Put it back on the hanger.
11. Hang it up and try on another one.
12. This one fits. Buy it.

Key Vocabulary

- near at hand: 가까운 장래에, 근처에 있는
- need to~: ~해야 한다, 할 필요가 있다
- look in ~: ~안을 들여다 보다
- go inside: 안으로 들어가다
- take off: 내리다, 떼어내다, 벗다
- rack: 걸대
- hanger: 옷걸이
- look at yourself: 자신을 보다
- hang up: 걸어놓다
- try on: 입어보다
- another one: 다른 것
- fit: (사이즈가) 맞다

B

1. Winter is near at ________.
2. You need to ______ a new coat.
3. ________ in the store windows.
4. Oh, there's a nice coat! Go _________.
5. Take a coat off the ________.
6. Take it _______ the hanger and try it _____.
7. Look at _____________ in the mirror.
8. Oh, it's too big. It's not your ________.
9. _________ it off.
10. Put it ________ on the hanger.
11. Hang it up and try on ___________ one.
12. This one ________. Buy it.

C

1. 겨울이 다가왔습니다.
2. 당신은 새 코트를 하나 사야합니다.
3. 상점 윈도우 안을 들여다보세요.
4. 아, 저기 좋은 게 하나 있네요. 안으로 들어가세요.
5. 걸대에서 코트를 하나 내리세요.
6. 옷걸이에서 벗겨내어 입어보세요.
7. 거울 속의 당신을 들여다보세요.
8. 아, 너무 큽니다. 당신 사이즈가 아니군요.
9. 벗으세요.
10. 옷걸이에 도로 거세요.
11. 걸어놓고 다른 것을 입어보세요.
12. 이건 맞습니다. 사세요.

66 Making a Grocery List

A

1. Make a list of groceries that you need.
2. Don't forget butter.
3. Erase "sugar". You have enough sugar.
4. Cross out "candy". You don't need candy.
5. Underline "meat" so that you won't forget it.
6. Circle "bread". That's important.
7. Print "MILK" in big letters.
8. What a messy list. Start over.
9. List only the things you really need.
10. That's better.
11. Cross out the first list.
12. Take your list to the grocery store.
13. Don't forget your money.

Key Vocabulary

- make a list: 목록을 작성하다
- grocery: 식료품
- forget: 잊다, 까먹다
- erase: 지우다
- enough: 충분한
- cross out: 줄을 그어 지우다
- underline: 밑줄을 긋다
- so that ~: ~하기 위해
- won't(=will not) ~: ~하지 않을 것이다
- circle: 동그라미 치다
- print: (활자체로) 쓰다
- big letter(=capital letter): 대문자
- messy: 지저분한
- start over: 다시 시작하다
- really: 정말로
- take A to B: A를 B로 가져가다
- grocery store: 식료품 상점

B

1. ________ a list of groceries that you need.
2. Don't ________ butter.
3. ________ "sugar". You have enough sugar.
4. ________ out "candy". You don't need candy.
5. Underline "meat" _______ that you won't forget it.
6. Circle "bread". That's important.
7. Print "MILK" in ______ letters.
8. What a __________ list. Start over.
9. List only the things you ________ need.
10. That's better.
11. Cross ______ the first list.
12. Take your list ___ the grocery store.
13. Don't _________ your money.

C

1. 당신이 필요로 하는 식료품 목록을 만드세요.
2. 버터를 잊지 마세요.
3. 설탕은 지우세요. 충분히 있습니다.
4. 사탕은 그어버리세요. 사탕은 필요 없습니다.
5. 잊지 않도록 고기에 밑줄을 그으세요.
6. 빵에 동그라미 치세요. 중요합니다.
7. 우유는 대문자로 쓰세요.
8. 목록이 엉망이네요! 다시 하세요.
9. 꼭 필요한 것만 적으세요.
10. 훨씬 낫네요.
11. 먼저 작성한 목록은 그어버리세요.
12. 작성한 목록을 식료품 상점으로 가져가세요.
13. 돈(가져가는 것)을 잊지 마세요.

67 Grocery Shopping

A

1. You're in a store for grocery shopping.
2. Go to the produce section.
3. Choose some fruit and put it in your cart.
4. Choose some vegetables and weigh them.
5. That's too much. Put some of them back.
6. Now, go to the dairy section

7. Choose some eggs.
8. That's enough food.
   Go to the check-out counter.

9. Stand in line and wait.
10. Now, your turn. Say "Hello." to the cashier.
11. Pay her/him for your groceries.
12. Wait for her/him to bag them.
13. Pick up your bag of groceries and go home.

Key Vocabulary

- grocery shopping: 식료품 장보기
- produce section: 농산물 구역
- cart: (쇼핑)카트
- weigh: 무게를 달다
- too much: 너무 많은
- put back: 도로 내놓다
- dairy section: 낙농제품 구역
- check-out counter: 계산대
- stand in line: 줄을 서다
- turn: 차례, 순서
- cashier: 계산원
- pay A for B: A에게 B의 값을 지불하다
- bag: 봉투에 담다
- pick up: 집어 들다

B

1. You're in a store for __________ shopping.
2. Go to the ___________ section.
3. Choose some fruit and put it in your _______.
4. Choose some vegetables and _______ them.
5. That's ______ much. Put some of them ________.
6. Now, go to the ________ section.
7. _________ some eggs.
8. That's _________ food.
   Go to the ____________ counter.
9. Stand in ________ and wait.
10. It's your turn. Say "Hello." to the ________.
11. Pay her/him _____ your groceries.
12. Wait for her/him to ______ them.
13. _______ up your bag of groceries and go home.

C

1. 당신은 식료품 장을 보기 위해 상점에 있습니다.
2. 농산물 구역으로 가세요.
3. 과일을 좀 골라서 카트에 담으세요.
4. 야채를 좀 골라서 무게를 다세요.
5. 너무 많습니다. 도로 좀 내려 놓으세요.
6. 이제, 낙농제품 구역으로 가세요.
7. 달걀을 좀 고르세요.
8. 그 정도면 충분한 음식입니다. 계산대로 가세요.
9. 줄을 서서 기다리세요.
10. 당신 차례입니다. 계산원에게 인사하세요.
11. 그/그녀에게 식료품 값을 지불하세요.
12. 봉투에 담을 때까지 기다리세요.
13. 식료품 봉투를 집어 들고 집으로 가세요.

68 Paying for Your Purchase

A

1. You purchased less than ten items at the grocery store.
2. Stand in line at the express line.
3. It's quick. Soon it's your turn.
4. The cashier rings up your purchases.
5. He/She presses the keys on the cash register.

6. He/She tells you the total amount to pay.
7. Take some money out of your purse and give it to him/her.
8. He/She puts the money into the register and takes out the change.
9. He/She gives you the receipt and the change.
10. Take the receipt and change.
11. Examine the items and prices on the receipt.
12. Everything is correct. Leave the store.

Key Vocabulary

- purchase: 사다 (=buy)
- express line: 빨리 계산하는 줄
- quick: 재빠른
- ring up the purchase: 구매품을 (센서기에 대어) 소리를 울리다 (계산하다)
- put A into B: A를 B 속에 넣다
- take out: 꺼내다
- leave: 떠나다
- receipt: 영수증
- less than ~: ~보다 적은
- item: 항목
- soon: 곧, 얼마 지나지 않아
- total amount: 총금액
- cash register: 현금등록기
- take A out of B: A를 B에서 꺼내다
- examine: 살펴보다
- change: 거스름돈, 잔돈
- correct: 정확한

B

1. You purchased less ______ ten items at the grocery store.
2. Stand in line at the __________ line.
3. It's ________. Soon it's your turn.
4. The ________ rings up your purchases.

5. He/She presses the keys on the cash ____________.
6. He/She tells you the total __________ to pay.

7. Take some money ______ of your purse and give it to him/her.
8. He/She puts the money into the register and takes out the __________.
9. He/She gives you the __________ and the change.
10. Take the receipt and change.
11. ________ the items and prices on the receipt.
12. Everything is __________. Leave the store.

C

1. 당신은 식료품점에서 10개 항목 이하로 샀습니다.
2. 급행 줄에 서세요.
3. 빠릅니다. 곧 당신 차례입니다.
4. 계산원이 당신이 산 물건들을 센서에 울립니다.
5. 그/그녀가 현금등록기의 키들을 누릅니다.
6. 그/그녀는 당신에게 총지불 금액을 말합니다.
7. 지갑에서 돈을 좀 꺼내어 그/그녀에게 주세요.
8. 그/그녀는 돈을 등록기에 넣고 거스름돈을 꺼냅니다.
9. 그/그녀는 영수증과 거스름돈을 당신에게 줍니다.
10. 영수증과 거스름돈을 받으세요.
11. 영수증에 있는 항목과 가격을 살펴보세요.
12. 모두 맞습니다. 상점을 떠나세요.

69 Cancelling a Purchase

A

1. You've been looking for a new bed for a long time.
2. Then, you got an ad for a big sale at a furniture store.
3. Go to the store and see different kinds of beds.
4. Ask the salesman when it'll be delivered.
5. The salesman says it'll be delivered in five days.
6. Sign the contract and leave for home.
7. When you get home, the phone is ringing.

8. Your mom tells you that she ordered a new bed for you and will be delivered soon.

9. Oh, no! You can't have two beds!
10. Call the furniture store and ask if you can cancel the purchase.
11. The salesman says, "No problem. You can cancel the purchase within 72 hours."
12. Say "I'm so sorry and cancel your purchase.

Key Vocabulary

- look for ~: ~을 찾다
- furniture store: 가구점
- salesman: 판매원
- contract: 계약서
- leave for ~: ~을 향해 떠나다
- soon: 곧, 머지않아
- no problem: 문제없다, 상관없다
- ad(=advertisement): 광고
- kind: 종류
- deliver: 배달하다
- in five days: 닷새 후에
- The phone is ringing.: 전화가 울리고 있다.
- cancel the purchase: 구매를 취소하다
- within ~: ~이내에

B

1. You've been looking _____ a new bed for a long time.
2. Then, you got an _____ for a big sale at a furniture store.
3. Go to the store and see different ________ of beds.
4. Ask the salesman when it'll be _____________.
5. The salesman says it'll be delivered _____ five days.
6. Sign the __________ and leave ______ home.
7. When you get home, the phone is __________.

8. Your mom tells you that she _________ a new bed for you and will be delivered soon.

9. Oh, no! You can't have two beds!
10. Call the furniture store and ask if you can ________ the purchase.
11. The salesman says, "No problem. You can cancel the purchase ________ 72 hours."
12. Say "I'm so sorry." and __________ your purchase.

C

1. 당신은 오랫동안 새 침대를 찾고 있었습니다.
2. 그러다 가구점에서 큰 세일이 있다는 광고를 접했습니다.
3. 가구점에 가서 다양한 종류의 가구를 보세요.
4. 언제 배달되는지 판매원에게 물어보세요.
5. 다음날 배달될 거라고 판매원이 말합니다.
6. 계약서에 사인을 하고 집으로 가세요.
7. 집에 도착했을 때 전화가 울립니다.
8. 당신의 어머니께서 당신을 위해 침대를 하나 샀으며 곧 배달될 거라고 하십니다.
9. 이런! 침대를 두 개 가질 수는 없습니다!
10. 가구점에 전화해서 구매한 것을 취소할 수 있는지 물어보세요.
11. 판매원이 “문제없어요. 72시간 이내에 취소할 수 있습니다.”라고 말합니다.
12. 대단히 미안하다고 말하고 구매를 취소하세요.

70 A Cashier

A

1. You're a cashier.
2. A customer wants you to change a ten-dollar bill.
3. Take the ten.
4. Count the change and give it to him/her.

5. Another customer wants to cash a check.

6. Ask her/him for her/his I.D.:
   "May I see your driver's license and a credit card?"
7. Look at her/his driver's license and credit card.
8. Look at the back of the check, copy the license number and the date of birth.
9. Write down the name of the company and the number of the credit card.

10. Count the cash and give it to the customer.

Key Vocabulary

- cashier: 계산원
- change: 바꾸다, 잔돈
- take: 받다
- cash a check: 수표를 현금으로 바꾸다
- driver's license: 운전면허증
- back: 뒷면
- look at: 보다
- credit card: 신용카드
- customer: 고객
- a ten-dollar bill: 10달러 지폐
- count: 세다, 헤아리다
- ask A for B: A에게 B를 요구하다
- I.D. (identification): 신분증
- copy: 베끼다
- date of birth: 생년월일

B

1. You're a __________.
2. A __________ wants you to change a ten-dollar bill.
3. Take the ten.
4. Count the change and give it to him/her.

5. ________ customer wants to ________ a check.

6. Ask her/him ______ her/his I.D.:
   "May I see your driver's __________ and a credit card?"
7. Look ____ her/his driver's license and credit card.
8. Look at the back of the check, __________ the license number and the date of ________.
9. Write _______ the name of the company and the number of the credit card.
10. Count the cash and give it to the customer.

C

1. 당신은 계산원입니다.
2. 한 고객이 10달러 지폐를 바꿔달라고 합니다.
3. 10달러를 받으세요.
4. 잔돈을 세서 그/그녀에게 주세요.
5. 또 다른 고객이 수표를 현금으로 바꿔달라고 합니다.
6. 그/그녀에게 신분증을 요구하세요.
   "운전면허증과 신용카드를 볼 수 있을까요?"
7. 그/그녀의 운전면허증과 신용카드를 보세요.
8. 수표 뒷면을 보고, 운전면허증 번호와 생년월일을 베껴놓으세요.
9. 신용카드의 회사이름과 번호를 적으세요.
10. 현금을 세서 고객에게 주세요.

71 Buying a plane Ticket

A

1. You plan to go to Hawaii this winter.
2. Go to a travel agency nearby.
3. Tell the clerk that you want a round-trip ticket to Hawaii.

4. The clerk asks you when you want to leave and come back.
5. Tell him/her that the departure date is December 10 and arrival date is February 20.

6. He/she says "What a long stay! Let me check the seats for you."
7. After a while, he/she tells you the available seats.
8. Choose the seats by the window.
9. He/She asks you for a credit card for booking.
10. Give him/her your credit card.
11. O.K. You're all set. Take your credit card back and return home.

Key Vocabulary

- travel agency: 여행사
- nearby: 근처
- round-trip ticket: 왕복여행 항공권
- departure date: 출발일
- long stay: 오래 머무름
- arrival date: 도착일
- let me ~: ~하겠습니다.
- available seats: 가능한 좌석, 구할 수 있는 좌석
- booking: 표 발행
- take back: 다시 가지다

B

1. You plan to go to Hawaii this winter.
2. Go to a travel __________ nearby.

3. Tell the clerk that you want a ________ ticket to Hawaii.
4. The clerk asks you _____ you want to leave and come back.
5. Tell him/her that the _______ date is December 10 and ____ date is February 20.

6. He/she says "_________ a long stay! Let me check the seats for you."
7. After a while, he/she tells you the __________ seats.
8. __________ the seats by the window.
9. He/She asks you _____ a credit card for __________.
10. Give him/her your credit card.
11. O.K. You're all set. Take your credit card _______ and return home.

C

1. 당신은 이번 겨울에 하와이로 갈 계획입니다.
2. 근처에 있는 여행사로 가세요.
3. 직원에게 하와이행 왕복표를 사고 싶다고 말하세요.
4. 직원이 언제 출발하고 돌아올지를 물어봅니다.
5. 출발일은 12월 10일이고 도착일은 2월 20일이라고 말하세요.
6. "오래 머무시네요! 좌석을 알아볼게요."라고 직원이 말합니다.
7. 잠시 후 직원이 가능한 좌석을 얘기해줍니다.
8. 창가 좌석들을 선택하세요.
9. 직원이 표를 끊기 위해 신용카드를 요구합니다.
10. 그에게 신용카드를 주세요.
11. 자, 다 됐습니다. 신용카드를 돌려받은 후 집으로 가세요.

72 Using an ATM

A

1. You need some cash for shopping.
2. Go to an ATM nearby.
3. Take your cash card out of your purse.
4. Line up the magnetic strip properly.
5. Insert the card into the slot on the ATM.
6. A message on the screen asks for your PIN.
7. Enter your PIN by pressing keys on the keypad.
8. Enter the amount of money you need.
9. The machine returns your card and money.
10. Don't forget to take both of them back!

* ATM: Automatic Teller Machine
* PIN: Personal Identification Number

Key Vocabulary

- cash: 현금
- nearby: 근처의, 근처에 있는
- cash card: 현금 카드
- line up: 바로 세우다
- properly: 적절히
- insert A into B: A를 B 속에 삽입하다
- PIN: 개인신분증명번호
- enter: 입력하다
- keypad: 키패드(키를 입력하는 작은 상자 모양의 것)
- ATM: 자동현금인출기
- take A out of B: A를 B에서 꺼내다
- magnetic strip: (자동해독을 위한) 자기 띠
- slot: 가는 틈, 투입구
- ask for ~: ~을 요구하다
- press keys: 키들을 누르다

B

1. You need some ______ for shopping.
2. Go to an ATM near your _________.
3. _______ your cash card out of your purse.
4. Line up the magnetic _______ properly.
5. Insert the card into the _______ on the ATM.
6. A message on the screen asks _____ your PIN.
7. Enter your PIN by pressing keys on the __________.
8. Enter the _________ of money you need.
9. The machine __________ your card and money.
10. Don't forget to _______ both of them back!

* ATM: Automatic Teller Machine
* PIN: Personal Identification Number

C

1. 당신은 장을 보기 위해서 현금이 좀 필요합니다.
2. 집 근처의 자동현금인출기로 가세요.
3. 지갑에서 현금카드를 끄집어내세요.
4. 자기 띠를 적절하게 손에 쥐세요.
5. 카드를 자동현금인출기의 투입구에 끼워 넣으세요.
6. 스크린의 메시지가 비밀번호를 넣으라고 합니다.
7. 키패드의 번호들을 눌러서 비밀번호를 입력합니다.
8. 당신이 원하는 만큼의 돈을 입력하세요.
9. 기계가 당신의 현금 카드와 돈을 돌려줍니다.
10. 둘 다 반드시 돌려받으세요!

SECTION 6

Travel & Transportation

73 Taking a Plane

A

1. You're going to New York.
2. Get on the plane and look for your seat number.
3. There it is! Sit down and fasten your seatbelt.
4. It's too tight. Loosen it.
5. Oh, this time it's too loose. Tighten it.
6. O.K. Here we go!
7. We're taking off.
8. Now we are flying through the air.
9. Enjoy your flight.
10. Have a good time in New York and safe return home!

Key Vocabulary

- get on: 올라타다
- look for: 찾다
- There it is!: 저기 있네!
- fasten seatbelt: 안전벨트를 매다
- tight: 꽉 죄는
- loosen: 느슨하게 하다
- fasten: 착용하다
- tighten: 꽉 죄다
- Here we go!: 자, 됐습니다!
- take off: 이륙하다
- fly through ~: ~를 통과하며 날다
- flight: 비행
- have a good time: 즐겁게 지내다
- safe return home: 집으로 안전하게 돌아오다

B

1. You're going to New York.
2. _____ on the plane and look ______ your seat number.
3. There it is! Sit down and _________ your seatbelt.
4. It's too ______. _________ it.
5. Oh, this time it's too loose. _________ it.

6. O.K. Here we _____!
7. We're taking _____.
8. Now we are flying ________ the air.

9. Enjoy your ______________.
10. ______ a good time in New York and safe _____ home!

C

1. 당신은 뉴욕에 가려고 합니다.
2. 비행기에 올라서 당신의 좌석을 찾으세요.
3. 저기 있네요! 앉아서 안전벨트를 매세요.
4. 너무 꽉 죄었어요. 느슨하게 하세요.
5. 아, 이번에는 너무 느슨합니다. 꽉 죄세요.
6. 좋습니다. 됐습니다.
7. 이륙을 합니다.
8. 이제 하늘을 날고 있습니다.
9. 비행을 즐기세요.
10. 뉴욕에서 재미있게 지내고 안전하게 집으로 돌아오세요.

74 A Rough Bus Ride

A

1. You're waiting for the bus.
2. Oh! Here it comes! Get on the bus.
3. Touch the card reader with your access card.
4. Go to an empty seat.
5. Gosh! This driver is terrible! Fall down.
6. Get up and tell the driver to take it easy.

7. Sit down. Look out of the window.
8. Bounce up and down.
9. Watch for your street.
10. There it is! Ring the bell.

11. Get off the bus through the back door.
12. Say "Whew! What a ride!"

Key Vocabulary

- wait for ~: ~을 기다리다
- get on ~: ~에 올라타다
- access card: 승차 카드
- Gosh!: 이런! 아이쿠!
- fall down: 넘어지다
- take it easy: 점잖게 하다, 편안하게 하다
- watch for~: ~을 잘 살피다
- There it is!: 저기 있네!
- get off ~ : ~에서 내리다
- back door: 뒷문 (cf. front door: 앞문)
- What a ride!: 무슨 이런 차가 있어!
- Here it comes: 여기 온다.
- card reader: 카드 읽는 기계
- empty seat: 빈 좌석
- terrible: 지독한, 형편없는
- get up: 일어나다
- look out of~: ~밖을 쳐다보다
- bounce up and down: 아래위로 튕기다
- ring the bell: 벨을 누르다

B

1. You're waiting ________ the bus.
2. Oh! ________ it comes! ________ on the bus.
3. Touch the card ________ with your ___________ card.
4. Go to an ________ seat.
5. Gosh! This driver is terrible! ________ down.

6. Get ______ and tell the driver to take it ________.
7. Sit down. Look _______ of the window.
8. _________ up and down.

9. Watch _______ your street.
10. _________ it is! Ring the bell.
11. Get off the bus through the _________ door.
12. Say "Whew! ________ a ride!"

C

1. 당신은 버스를 기다리고 있습니다.
2. 아, 여기 오네요! 버스에 올라타세요.
3. 승차 카드를 요금 기계에 대세요.
4. 빈 자리로 가세요.
5. 아이쿠! 운전사가 형편없네요! 넘어졌군요.
6. 일어나서 운전사에게 좀 점잖게 운전하라고 말하세요.
7. 앉으세요. 창밖을 내다보세요.
8. 아래위로 튀어 오릅니다.
9. 당신이 내릴 거리를 잘 살피세요.
10. 저기 있네요. 벨을 누르세요.
11. 뒷문을 통해 내리세요.
12. "휴, 무슨 이런 차가 있어!"라고 말하세요.

75 A Car Ride

A

1. You're going to take a ride in your car.
2. Take out your car key and unlock the car.
3. Open the door, get in and start the engine.
4. Release the hand brake.
5. Put the car in first gear and drive away.
6. Change to second gear.

7. Speed up and shift into third.
8. Uh-oh! Too fast! Here comes a policeman.
9. Pull over to the side of the street and stop.
10. Roll down the window, and say "I'm sorry, officer."
11. Start to cry.
12. That did it! He's not giving you a ticket this time.
13. But you got a warning. Be careful!

Key Vocabulary

- take a ride: 차를 타다
- unlock: 열다, 잠금장치를 풀다
- release: 풀다
- drive away: 운전해서 떠나가다
- change to ~: ~로 바꾸다
- shift into ~: ~로 바꾸다
- roll down the window: 창문을 내리다
- give a ticket: 위반딱지를 받다
- Be careful!: 조심하세요!
- take out: 꺼내다
- get in: (승용차에) 올라타다
- put the car in the first gear: 자동차 기어를 1단에 놓다
- speed up: 속도를 내다
- pull over to the side of the street: 갓길로 대다
- That did it!: 통했다!
- get a warning: 경고를 받다

B

1. You're going to take a _______ in your car.
2. _______ out your car key and ________ the car.
3. Open the door, get _____ and start the engine.
4. __________ the hand brake.
5. Put the car in first gear and drive _____.

6. Change _____ second gear.
7. Speed _____ and ________ into third.
8. Uh-oh! Too fast! Here ________ a policeman.
9. Pull _______ to the side of the street and stop.
10. Roll ________ the window, and say "I'm sorry, officer."
11. Start to cry.
12. That _____ it! He's not giving you a _______ this time.
13. But you got a ___________. Be careful!

C

1. 당신은 차를 운전하려 합니다.
2. 차 키를 꺼내서 차를 여세요.
3. 문을 열고 들어가서 시동을 거세요.
4. 핸드브레이크를 푸세요.
5. 기어를 1단에 놓고 운전해 나가세요.
6. 2단으로 바꾸세요.
7. 속도를 올리고 3단으로 바꾸세요.
8. 아이고! 너무 빠릅니다. 경찰이 오네요.
9. 갓길로 대고 멈추세요.
10. 창문을 내리고, "경찰관님, 죄송합니다."라고 말하세요.
11. 울기 시작하세요.
12. 통했네요! 그가 이번에는 위반딱지를 받지 않았어요.
13. 하지만 당신은 경고를 받았습니다. 조심하세요!

76 Cleaning a Car

A

1. Your car is dirty and you need to clean it.
2. First, clean the inside of the windows.
3. Then, wipe off the dashboard and vacuum the floor.
4. The inside of the car is clean.
5. Now, dip a sponge into soapy water.
6. Wash the outside of the car with it.
7. Rinse the car by spraying it with water .
8. Dry the car with a rag.
9. Spread some wax on the car.
10. Wipe the wax off.
11. Buff the car with a soft cloth.
12. Wow! The car looks like a brand new one!

Key Vocabulary

- inside: 안쪽
- dashboard: 계기판
- floor: 바닥
- soapy water: 비눗물
- rinse: 헹구다
- rag: 걸레
- buff: 문지르다, 닦다
- brand new: 완전한 새것의
- wipe off: 닦아내다
- vacuum: 진공청소기로 청소하다
- dip A into B: A를 B에 담그다
- outside: 바깥쪽
- spray: 뿌리다
- spread: 펼치다, 펼쳐 바르다
- look like ~: ~처럼 보이다

B

1. Your car is dirty and you need to clean it.
2. First, clean the __________ of the windows.
3. Then, wipe off the ___________ and vacuum the floor.
4. The inside of the car is clean.
5. Now, dip a sponge into _________ water.
6. Wash the ___________ of the car with it.
7. ________ the car by spraying it with water.
8. _______ the car with a rag.
9. __________ some wax on the car.
10. Wipe the wax _______.
11. _________ the car with a soft cloth.
12. Wow! The car looks like a __________ new one!

C

1. 당신의 차가 더러워서 청소를 해야 합니다.
2. 먼저 유리창 안쪽을 닦으세요.
3. 다음으로 계기판을 닦고 바닥을 진공청소기로 청소하세요.
4. 차 안쪽은 깨끗합니다.
5. 이제, 스펀지를 비눗물에 적시세요.
6. 그것으로 차 바깥을 씻으세요.
7. 물을 뿌려서 차를 헹구세요.
8. 헝겊조각으로 차의 물기를 닦으세요.
9. 왁스를 좀 펴 바르세요.
10. 왁스를 닦아내세요.
11. 부드러운 천으로 문지르세요.
12. 와! 차가 완전 새것 같아요!

77 Taking a bus

A

1. You're going to take a bus.
2. Walk to the bus stop.
3. Sit on the bench and wait for the bus.

4. The bus runs every ten minutes and it arrives on time.
5. Here comes the bus! Get on the bus through the front door.

6. Touch the card reader with your access card.
7. All the seats are taken. Stand in the aisle.
8. Hold on to a strap on the overhead bars.
9. Soon, a passenger gets off the bus and a seat is empty.
10. Go to the empty seat and sit down.
11. Now your stop is near. Press the stop button.
12. The bus stops. Go to the back door and get off.

Key Vocabulary

- take a bus: 버스를 타다
- bus stop: 버스정류장
- wait for~: ~을 기다리다
- run: 운행하다
- every ten minutes: 10분마다
- get on: 올라타다
- through ~: ~을 통하여
- front door: 앞문
- card reader: 카드 인식기
- access card: 통과 카드
- aisle: 통로, 복도
- hold on to~: ~을 꽉 붙들다
- strap: 가죽 손잡이
- overhead bars: 머리 위 지지대
- passenger: 승객
- empty: 비어있는, 빈
- stop button: 정지 버튼
- back door: 뒷문
- get off: 내리다
- All the seats are taken.: 모든 좌석이 찼다.

B

1. You're going to ________ a bus.
2. Walk to the bus ________.
3. Sit on the bench and wait __ the bus.
4. The bus _______ every ten minutes and it arrives ______ time.

5. Here comes the bus! Get on the bus through the ________ door.
6. Touch the card __________ with your access card.
7. All the seats are ______. Stand in the ________.
8. Hold on to a _______ on the _________ bars.
9. Soon, a _________ gets off the bus and a seat is ______.
10. Go to the _________ seat and sit down.
11. Now your ________ is near. Press the stop button.
12. The bus stops. Go to the ______ door and get off.

C

1. 당신은 버스를 타려합니다.
2. 버스정류장으로 걸어가세요.
3. 벤치에 앉아서 버스를 기다리세요.
4. 버스는 10분마다 운행하고 제 시각에 도착합니다.
5. 버스가 옵니다! 앞문을 통해서 버스에 올라타세요.
6. 통행 카드를 카드 인식기에 대세요.
7. 모든 좌석이 찼습니다. 통로에 서세요.
8. 머리 위 지지대에 붙어있는 가죽 손잡이를 꽉 잡으세요.
9. 곧, 한 승객이 버스에서 내리고 자리가 하나 비었습니다.
10. 빈 자리로 가서 앉으세요.
11. 이제 당신이 내릴 정류장에 다 왔습니다. 정지 버튼을 누르세요.
12. 버스가 멈춥니다. 뒷문으로 가서 내리세요.

78 Taking a Train

A

1. You're going to visit your family in your hometown.
2. Go to the train station.
3. All the ticket windows are crowded with passengers.

4. Go to the ticket machine and buy a ticket.
5. It's quick!
6. Insert your ticket into the slot in the turnstile.
7. The gate opens. Walk through the gate.
8. Wait on the platform next to the track.

9. Your train arrives. Get on.
10. Find your seat and sit down.
11. Enjoy the view outside during the ride.

Key Vocabulary

- train station: 기차역
- ticket window: 매표소
- crowded with ~: ~로 붐비는
- passenger: 승객
- ticket machine: 표 판매기
- quick: 재빠른
- insert A into B: A를 B에 넣다
- slot: 가는 틈, 투입구
- turnstile: 회전문
- walk through: 걸어서 통과하다
- platform: 승강구
- next to ~: ~옆의
- track: 철로, 선로
- view: 경치, 전망
- during ~: ~동안
- ride: 타고 가다

B

1. You're going to visit your family in your hometown.
2. Go to the train ________.
3. All the ticket _________ are crowded with ___________.
4. Go to the ticket machine and buy a ticket.
5. It's __________!
6. _______ your ticket into the slot in the _________.

7. The gate opens. Walk through the gate.
8. Wait on the _________ next to the ________.
9. Your train __________. Get on.
10. _________ your seat and sit down.
11. Enjoy the view outside during the ___________.

C

1. 당신은 고향에 있는 가족을 방문하려 합니다.
2. 기차역으로 가세요.
3. 모든 매표소가 승객들로 붐빕니다.
4. 표 판매기로 가서 표를 한 장 사세요.
5. 정말 빠르네요!
6. 회전문의 투입구에 표를 넣으세요.
7. 문이 열립니다. 걸어서 문을 통과하세요.
8. 선로 바로 옆의 승강장에서 기다리세요.
9. 당신이 탈 기차가 도착합니다. 올라타세요.
10. 자리를 찾아서 앉으세요.
11. 타고 가는 동안 바깥 경치를 구경하세요.

79 Taking a Taxi

A

1. You are in a hurry and have to take a taxi.
2. Hail a taxi and a taxi stops.
3. Get into the back seat.
4. Tell the driver where to go.

5. The driver starts the meter.
6. Check the meter.
7. During the ride, give the driver directions.

8. Tell him where to stop.
9. The car stops where you want.
10. Check the meter and pay the fare.
11. Give the driver a tip.
12. The driver says "Thank you." and drives away.

Key Vocabulary

- in a hurry: 서두르는, 급한
- take a taxi: 택시를 타다
- hail a taxi: 손을 흔들어 택시를 부르다
- get into ~: ~에 들어가다, 타다
- back seat: 뒷좌석 (cf. front seat: 앞좌석)
- during the ride: 타고 가는 동안
- give directions: 방향을 안내하다
- where to stop: 멈출 장소, 곳
- pay the fare: 요금을 지불하다
- give a tip: 팁을 주다
- drive away: (운전해서) 떠나가다

B

1. You are in a ________ and have to take a taxi.
2. ________ a taxi and a taxi stops.
3. Get into the ________ seat.
4. Tell the driver ________ to go.

5. The driver ________ the meter.
6. Check the meter.
7. During the ________, give the driver ________.
8. Tell him ________ to stop.

9. The car stops ________ you want.
10. Check the meter and pay the ________.
11. Give the driver a ________.
12. The driver says "Thank you." and ________ away.

C

1. 당신은 급해서 택시를 타야 합니다.
2. 손을 흔들어 택시를 부르고 택시가 섭니다.
3. 뒷좌석에 타세요.
4. 운전사에게 갈 곳을 얘기하세요.
5. 운전사가 미터기를 시작합니다.
6. 미터기를 체크하세요.
7. 타고 가는 동안 운전사에게 방향을 안내하세요.
8. 멈출 곳을 얘기하세요.
9. 차가 당신이 원하는 곳에 멈춥니다.
10. 미터기를 확인하고 요금을 내세요.
11. 운전사에게 팁을 주세요.
12. 운전사가 "감사합니다!"라고 말하고 떠나갑니다.

80 Taking a Subway Train

A

1. Go to the subway station.
2. Check the route and the fare
3. Buy a ticket from the ticket machine.
4. Insert the ticket into the slot in the turnstile.
5. The gate opens and the ticket comes out.
6. Take your ticket back and walk through the gate.
7. Go to the platform next to the track.
8. Here comes the train. Get on the train.
9. The train is so crowded.
10. Hold on to a stripe on overhead bars.
11. Finally, your station is announced.
12. Get off the train.

Key Vocabulary

- subway station: 지하철역
- route: 노선
- fare: 요금
- ticket machine: 매표기
- insert A into B: A를 B에 넣다
- slot: 가는 틈, 투입구
- turnstile: 회전문
- come out: 나오다
- take back: 다시 찾다
- platform: 승강장
- next to ~: ~옆의
- track: 선로
- Here comes ~!: ~이 온다!
- stripe: (가죽) 손잡이
- so crowded: 아주 복잡한 (=very crowded)
- hold on to ~: ~을 꽉 잡다
- overhead bars: 머리 위 지지대

B

1. Go to the subway ____________.

2. Check the ________ and the ________.
3. Buy a _______ from the ticket machine.
4. _________ the ticket into the slot in the __________.
5. The gate opens and the ticket comes ______.
6. _______ your ticket back and walk through the gate.
7. Go to the platform next to the __________.
8. ________ comes the train. Get on the train.
9. The train is so __________.
10. Hold on to a _________ on overhead bars.
11. Finally, your station is ___________.
12. Get ______ the train.

C

1. 지하철역으로 가세요.
2. 노선과 요금을 체크하세요.
3. 매표기에서 표를 사세요.
4. 표를 회전문의 투입구에 넣으세요.
5. 문이 열리고 표가 나옵니다.
6. 표를 다시 가지고 걸어서 문을 통과하세요.
7. 선로 옆에 있는 승강장으로 가세요.
8. 열차가 옵니다. 올라타세요.
9. 열차가 매우 복잡합니다.
10. 머리 위 지지대에 붙어 있는 손잡이를 꽉 잡으세요.
11. 마침내 당신이 내릴 역이 방송됩니다.
12. 열차에서 내리세요.

81 Changing a Flat Tire

A

1. Your car has a flat tire and you have to change it.
2. Take all the equipment out of the trunk.
3. Jack the car up.
4. Take off the flat tire.
5. Take the spare tire out of the trunk.
6. Put the spare tire on the wheel.
7. Tighten the lug nuts by hand.
8. Lower the car to the ground.
9. Tighten the nuts some more with a lug wrench.
10. Finally, put the hubcap on the wheel.
11. It's done.
12. Put all the equipment back in the trunk.

Key Vocabulary

- flat: 납작한
- take A out of B: A를 B에서 꺼내다
- take off: 벗겨내다, 빼내다
- wheel: 바퀴
- tighten: 죄다
- by hand: 손으로
- ground: 땅바닥
- wrench: 렌치, 나사 죄는 공구
- It's done: 다 됐다.
- flat tire: 구멍 난 타이어
- equipment: 장비, 기구
- jack up: 들어 올리다
- spare tire: 여분의 타이어
- put on: 끼우다, 씌우다
- lug nut: 돌출부 나사
- lower: 낮추다, 내리다
- some more: 좀더
- hubcap: 바퀴 덮개
- put back: 제자리에 다시 놓다

B

1. Your car has a ______ tire and you have to change it.
2. Take all the ___________ out of the trunk.
3. _________ the car up.
4. Take _______ the flat tire.
5. Take the _________ tire out of the trunk.

6. Put the spare tire _______ the wheel.
7. _________ the lug nuts by hand.
8. __________the car to the ground.
9. Tighten the nuts some more with a lug ___________.
10. Finally, put the __________ on the wheel.
11. It's ________.
12. Put all the equipment _______ in the trunk.

C

1. 당신 차의 타이어에 구멍이 나서 타이어를 바꿔야 합니다.
2. 트렁크에서 모든 필요한 장비들을 꺼내세요.
3. 잭으로 차를 들어 올리세요.
4. 구멍 난 타이어를 빼내세요.
5. 트렁크에서 여분의 타이어를 들어내세요.
6. 바퀴에 여분의 타이어를 끼우세요.
7. 돌출 부위 나사를 손으로 죄세요.
8. 차를 땅으로 내리세요.
9. 돌출 부위 나사 죄는 렌치로 나사를 좀더 죄세요.
10. 마지막으로, 바퀴 덮개를 바퀴에 씌우세요.
11. 다 됐습니다.
12. 모든 장비를 트렁크 속에 다시 넣으세요.

82 Picking Up a Friend

A

1. You're going to pick up your friend at the airport.
2. Drive your car to the airport.

3. Leave your car at the parking lot.
4. Go to the arrival area and check the monitor.
5. It says the flight has already arrived.
6. Wait for your friend to show up at the gate.

7. There he/she comes!
8. He/She carries two big bags.
9. Have him/her wait in front of the terminal and go get your car.
10. Stop your car in front of your friend.
11. Help him/her put the luggage in the trunk.

12. Get in the car and drive away.

Key Vocabulary

- pick up: 마중가다
- parking lot: 주차장
- monitor: (비행기 이착륙을 알려주는) 모니터
- wait for: 기다리다
- There he/she comes!: 저기 그/그녀가 오네!
- terminal: 터미널
- luggage: 짐
- drive away: (운전해서) 떠나가다
- leave: 남겨두다
- arrival area: 도착 장소 (cf. departure area: 출발 장소)
- flight: 비행기
- show up: 나타나다
- carry: 운반하다, 지니고 있다
- in front of ~: ~앞에
- go get: 가지러 가다
- get in: (승용차에) 타다

B

1. You're going to ________ up your friend at the airport.
2. Drive your car to the airport.

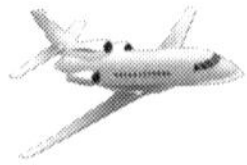

3. Leave your car at the parking ______.
4. Go to the ____________ area and check the monitor.
5. It says the _________ has already arrived.
6. Wait ______ your friend to ________ up at the gate.

7. There he/she comes!
8. He/She __________ two big bags.
9. Have him/her wait in ______ of the terminal and go _______ your car.
10. Stop your car in front of your friend.

11. Help him/her put the _________ in the trunk.
12. Get in the car and drive ________.

C

1. 당신은 공항에서 친구를 마중하려 합니다.
2. 공항으로 차를 운전해 가세요.
3. 주차장에 차를 주차하세요.
4. 도착 장소로 가서 모니터를 체크하세요.
5. 비행기가 이미 도착했다고 나옵니다.
6. 친구가 게이트에서 나올 때까지 기다리세요.
7. 저기 오네요!
8. 두 개의 큰 가방을 가지고 옵니다.
9. 터미널 앞에서 기다리게 하고 차를 가지러 가세요.
10. 친구 앞에서 차를 멈추세요.
11. 친구가 짐을 트렁크에 싣는 걸 도와주세요.
12. 차를 타고 운전해서 떠나세요.

83 Riding a Bike

A

1. You're going to ride a bike to work.
2. Put on your helmet.
3. Hold the handlebars.

4. Swing one of your legs over the bike and get on.
5. Start pedaling and the bike moves.
6. After a while, you met a hill.
7. Shift the gear into a lower one and go up the hill.
8. Now, you're coming down the hill.
   Squeeze the brakes to slow down.

9. Finally, you reached the parking place.
10. Get off your bike and lock it up in a bike rack.
11. Walk a few minutes to your destination.
12. What a good exercise!

Key Vocabulary

- ride a bike: 자전거를 타다
※ bike(=bicycle)
- work: 일, 직장
- hold: 쥐다, 잡다
- swing A over B: A를 B 위로 휘두르다
- start pedaling: 페달을 밟기 시작하다
- slow down: 속도를 줄이다
- parking place: 주차장
- lock up: 잠그다
- destination: 목적지
- helmet: 헬멧
- handlebar: (자전거) 핸들
- after a while: 얼마 후에
- shift A into B: A를 B로 바꾸다
- squeeze: 꽉 쥐다
- reach: 도달하다
- hill: 언덕
- come down: 내려오다
- get off: 내리다
- bike rack: 자전거 주차대
- exercise: 운동

B

1. You're going to _______ a bike to work.
2. Put _____ your helmet.
3. Hold the _________.

4. Swing one of your legs ______ the bike and get on.
5. Start pedaling and the bike _______.
6. After a while, you ______ a hill.
7. ______ the gear into a lower one and go ___ the hill.
8. Now, you're coming ________ the hill.
   Squeeze the brakes to _______ down.

9. Finally, you _________ the parking place.
10. Get off your bike and ______ it up in a bike _____.
11. Walk a few minutes to your ________________.
12. What a good ____________!

C

1. 당신은 직장에 자전거를 타고 가려합니다.
2. 헬멧을 쓰세요.
3. 핸들을 꽉 쥐세요.
4. 다리 한 짝을 자전거 위로 휘둘러서 자전거에 타세요.
5. 페달을 밟기 시작하고 자전거가 움직입니다.
6. 얼마 후 언덕을 만납니다.
7. 기어를 낮은 단계로 바꾸고 언덕을 올라가세요.
8. 이제, 언덕을 내려옵니다. 속도를 늦추기 위해 브레이크를 꽉 쥐세요.
9. 마침내, 당신은 주차장에 도달합니다.
10. 자전거에서 내려서 주차대에 자전거를 잠그세요.
11. 목적지까지 몇 분 걸으세요.
12. 참 좋은 운동이네요!

84 Driving a Car

A

1. It's a holiday and you want to enjoy driving.
2. Sit in the driver's seat.
3. Adjust your seat and the rear-view mirror.
4. Buckle your seat belt.
5. Step on the clutch pedal.

6. Put the key into ignition and turn it.
7. Shift the gear from P to D.
8. Take your foot off the clutch.
9. The car starts moving.

10. To go faster, press the accelerator.
11. To slow down, take your foot off the accelerator.
12. Roll down the window and enjoy your driving.

Key Vocabulary

- adjust: 맞추다, 조정하다
- buckle: (안전벨트를) 매다, 버클을 채우다
- ignition: 시동장치
- clutch pedal: 클러치 페달
- shift from P to D: '주차'에서 '운전'으로 바꾸다 (P: Parking 주차, D: driving 운전)
- rear-view mirror: 백미러
- put the key into ~: 열쇠를 ~에 꽂다
- step on: 밟다
- take A off B: A를 B에서 떼어 내다
- go faster; 더 빨리 가다
- accelerator: 가속장치
- slow down: 속도를 줄이다
- roll down the window: (돌려 감아서) 창을 내리다

B

1. It's a holiday and you want to enjoy driving.
2. Sit in the _______ seat.
3. ________ your seat and the ____________ mirror.
4. Buckle your seat _______.
5. Step on the _________ pedal.

6. Put the key into __________ and turn it.
7. ________ the gear from P to D.

8. Take your foot _______ the clutch.
9. The car starts _________.
10. To go faster, press the ______________.
11. To _______ down, take your foot off the accelerator.
12. _______ down the window and enjoy your driving.

C

1. 휴일이라 당신은 드라이빙을 하고 싶습니다.
2. 운전석에 앉으세요.
3. 좌석을 백미러를 조정하세요.
4. 안전벨트를 하세요.
5. 클러치 페달을 밟으세요.
6. 열쇠를 시동장치에 끼우고 돌리세요.
7. 기어를 P에서 D로 바꾸세요.
8. 클러치에서 빨을 떼세요.
9. 차가 움직이기 시작합니다.
10. 더 빨리 가기 위해서 가속장치를 밟으세요.
11. 속도를 늦추기 위해서 가속장치에서 발을 떼세요.
12. 창을 내리고 운전을 즐기세요.

85 At the Airport

A

1. Go to the airline check-in counter.
2. Present the attendant your passport and the e-ticket.
3. The attendant checks your passport and e-ticket.
4. The attendant confirms your destination, connecting flight, and the seats.

5. The attendant then puts your luggage on the scale.
6. O.K. Good! It doesn't go over the weight limit.
7. The attendant puts it on the conveyer belt.
8. The attendant asks you to stay around for a while until the inspection is over.
9. O.K. Everything's fine.
10. Now you can go to the gate for departure.

Key Vocabulary

- airline: 항공사
- present: 제출하다
- turn: 차례, 순서
- confirm: 확인하다
- e-ticket: 전자 티켓
- connecting flight: 연결 비행기
- scale: 저울
- go over: 넘다
- stay around: 근처에 머물다
- for a while: 한동안
- departure: 출발
- check-in counter: 탑승수속 카운터
- passport: 여권
- attendant: (항공사) 직원
- destination: 목적지
- luggage: 짐
- weight limit: 무게 제한
- conveyer belt: (자동으로 짐을 옮기는) 컨베이어벨트
- inspection: 검사

B

1. Go to the airline __________ counter.
2. __________ the attendant your passport and the e-ticket.
3. The attendant checks your passport and the e-ticket.
4. The attendant _________ your destination, ____________ flight, and the seats.

5. The attendant then puts your ________ on the scale.
6. O.K. Good! It doesn't go over the __________ limit.
7. The attendant puts it on the ___________ belt.
8. The attendant asks you to stay ________ for a while until the ___________ is over.

9. O.K. Everything's fine.
10. Now you can go to the gate for ___________.

C

1. 항공사 탑승수속 카운터로 가세요.
2. 복잡하네요. 줄을 서서 기다리세요.
3. 마침내 당신 차례입니다.
4. 직원에게 여권과 e-티켓을 제시하세요.
5. 직원이 당신의 여권과 e-티켓을 체크하고 당신의 목적지, 연결비행기, 그리고 좌석을 확인해줍니다.
6. 그러고 나서 직원은 당신의 짐을 저울에 올립니다.
7. 좋습니다! 무게 제한을 넘지 않았어요.
8. 직원이 당신의 짐을 컨베이어벨트 위에 놓습니다.
9. 직원이 당신에게 짐 검사를 하는 동안 근처에 있으라고 말합니다.
10. 모든 게 좋습니다. 이제 출발 게이트로 가도 좋습니다.

SECTION 7

Communication & Socializing

86 Calling a Friend

A

1. You have something to inform your friend.
2. You try to reach him/her, but the cell phone is off.
3. Call his/her home.
4. His/her mom answers the phone.
5. Say "Hello." to his/her mom and tell her who you are.
6. Ask her if your friend is available.
7. She says your friend is sick in bed.
8. Tell her that you are sorry.
9. She asks if you want to leave a message.
10. Say, "It's O.K. I'll call back later."
11. She says she will ask him/her to return your call.
12. Tell her that you appreciate it and hang up.

Key Vocabulary

- inform: 알리다
- off: 꺼진
- available: 전화받을 수 있는, 연결할 수 있는
- reach: 도달하다, 연락을 취하다
- who you are: 당신이 누구인지
- sick in bed: 아파서 누워있는
- sorry: 유감스러운
- leave a message: 메시지를 남기다
- call back later: 나중에 다시 전화하다
- return a call: 답신 전화를 하다
- appreciate: 감사하게 생각하다
- hang up: (전화를) 끊다

B

1. You have something to ______ your friend.
2. You try to _____ him/her, but the cell phone is ____.
3. Call his/her home.
4. His/her mom __________ the phone.
5. Say "Hello." to his/her mom and tell her ______ you are.
6. Ask her if your friend is __________.
7. She says your friend is sick ___ bed.
8. Tell her that you are ________.
9. She asks if you want to _____ a message.
10. Say, "It's O.K. I'll call ______ later."
11. She says she will ask him/her to ______ your call.
12. Tell her that you _________ it and hang up.

C

1. 당신은 한 친구에게 알려줄 게 있습니다.
2. 친구에게 연락을 하려고 애썼지만 휴대폰이 꺼져있습니다.
3. 그(녀)의 집으로 전화하세요.
4. 그(녀)의 어머니가 전화를 받습니다.
5. 그(녀)의 어머니께 "안녕하세요?"라고 인사하고 당신이 누군지 얘기하세요.
6. 친구가 있는지 물어보세요.
7. 그녀는 친구가 아파서 누워있다고 말합니다.
8. 그녀에게 유감을 표하세요.
9. 그녀는 남길 메시지가 있느냐고 묻습니다.
10. "괜찮습니다. 나중에 다시 걸겠습니다."라고 말하세요.
11. 그녀는 친구에게 전화를 걸어주라고 하겠다고 말합니다.
12. 그녀에게 감사하다고 얘기하고 전화를 끊으세요.

87 Making an International Call

A

1. You just arrived in the U.S. and want to make an international call to your mom at home.
2. Go to a gas station and get a calling card.
3. Scratch off the card for the ID number.
4. Now, you can see the ID number.
5. Go to a pay phone nearby.
6. Following the instruction on the card, press the ID number, country code, city code and your home phone number.
7. The phone rings and your mom answers the phone.
8. Your mom asks how everything's going.
9. Tell her that everything's just fine.
10. Your mom says she is relieved.
11. Say "I miss you, mom. I'll call again. Bye!" and hang up.

Key Vocabulary

- arrive in ~: ~에 도착하다
- gas station: 주유소
- calling card: 전화카드 (=phone card)
- nearby: 근처
- follow the instruction: 지시를 따르다
- be relieved: 안심되다
- make an international call: 국제전화를 걸다
- scratch off: 긁어내다
- ID number: (카드를 사용을 가능하게 하는) 승인번호
- how everything's going: 매사 어떤지
- miss: 보고 싶어하다, 그리워하다

B

1. You just arrived in the U.S. and want to __________ an international call to your mom at home.
2. Go to a gas station and get a _______ card.
3. Scratch _______ the card for the ID number.
4. Now, you can see the ID number.
5. Go to a pay phone __________.

6. Following the ________ on the card, press the ID number, country code, city code and your home phone number.
7. The phone _______ and your mom answers the phone.
8. Your mom asks ________ everything's going.
9. Tell her that everything's just fine.
10. Your mom says she is __________.
11. Say "I _______ you, mom. I'll call again. Bye!" and hang up.

C

1. 당신은 방금 미국에 도착해서 집에 계신 어머니께 국제 전화를 걸고 싶습니다.
2. 주유소로 가서 전화카드를 하나 구입하세요.
3. 승인번호를 얻기 위해 카드를 긁어보세요.
4. 자, 승인번호가 보입니다.
5. 근처의 공중전화로 가세요.
6. 카드에 있는 지시대로 승인번호, 국가번호, 지역번호, 집 전화번호를 누르세요.
7. 전화가 울리고 당신의 어머니께서 전화를 받습니다.
8. 어머니께서 어떠냐고 물으십니다.
9. 모든 게 좋다고 말씀드리세요.
10. 어머니는 안심이 된다고 말씀하십니다.
11. "어머니 보고 싶어요. 다시 전화 드릴께요. 안녕히 계세요!"라고 말씀드리고 전화를 끊으세요.

88 Using a Cell Phone

A

1. You want to make a call to your friend.
2. Pick up your cell phone.
3. Open the top.
4. Press the phone number and "send" button.
5. Your friend's phone is ringing.
6. Your friend answers the phone.
7. Say "Hi!" and talk to your friend.
8. Ask how things are going.
9. Make an appointment for the weekend.
10. Finally, your talk is over.
11. Say "Good-bye!" and press the "end" button.
12. Close the top.

Key Vocabulary

- cell phone: 휴대전화 (=mobile phone)
- make a call: 전화를 걸다
- pick up: 집어 들다
- "send" button: "보내기" 버튼
- ring: (전화벨이) 울리다
- how things are going: 어떻게 지내는지
- make an appointment: (시간)약속을 하다
- be over: 끝나다
- "end" button: 종료 버튼
- close the top: 뚜껑을 닫다

B

1. You want to ________ a call to your friend.
2. Pick ________ your cell phone.
3. Open the ________.
4. Press the phone number and "send" button.
5. Your friend's phone is ___________.
6. Your friend answers the phone.
7. Say "Hi!" and talk to your friend.
8. Ask ________ things are going.
9. Make an _____________ for the weekend.
10. Finally, your talk is ________.
11. Say "Good-bye!" and press the "end" button.
12. Close the ________.

C

1. 당신은 친구에게 전화를 걸고 싶습니다.
2. 휴대폰을 집어 드세요.
3. 뚜껑을 여세요.
4. 전화번호를 누르고 “보내기” 버튼을 누르세요.
5. 친구의 전화가 울립니다.
6. 친구가 전화를 받습니다.
7. 친구에게 “안녕!”하고 인사한 뒤 얘기하세요.
8. 어떻게 지내는지 물어보세요.
10. 마침내, 당신의 통화가 끝이 났습니다.
11. “잘 있어!”라고 말한 뒤 “종료” 버튼을 누르세요.
12. 뚜껑을 닫으세요.

89 Using a Pay Phone

A

1. You're going to make a phone call.
2. Go into the phone booth.
3. Pick up the receiver.
4. Take out a quarter.
5. Stick it in the slot.
6. Listen for the dial tone. You hear it.
7. Press the phone number.
8. It's busy. Hang up.
9. Get your quarter back.
10. Wait a few minutes.
11. Try again.
12. O.K. Good. This time it's ringing.
13. Talk to your friend.

Key Vocabulary

- make a (phone) call: 전화를 걸다
- phone booth: 전화 부스
- pick up: 집어 들다
- receiver: 수화기
- take out: 꺼내다
- stick A in B: A를 B에 끼워 넣다
- listen for ~: ~가 들리는지 듣다
- dial tone: 신호음
- It's busy.: 통화 중이다.
- hang up: 끊다
- get back: 돌려받다
- try again: 다시 시도하다
- It's ringing.: 신호가 가다. (전화가) 울리다.

B

1. You're going to ________ a phone call.
2. Go into the phone ________.
3. Pick ______ the receiver.
4. Take _______ a quarter.
5. Stick it in the ________.
6. Listen ________ the dial tone. You hear it.
7. Press the phone number.
8. It's ________. Hang up.
9. Get your quarter ________.
10. ________ a few minutes.
11. ________ again.
12. O.K. Good. This time it's __________.
13. Talk to your friend.

C

1. 당신은 전화를 걸려고 합니다.
2. 전화 부스로 들어가세요.
3. 수화기를 집어 드세요.
4. 25센트짜리 동전을 하나 꺼내세요.
5. 동전 구멍에 그것을 끼워 넣으세요.
6. 신호 가는 소리를 들으세요. 들리네요.
7. 전화번호를 누르세요.
8. 통화 중이네요. 끊으세요.
9. 동전을 돌려받으세요.
10. 몇 분 기다리세요.
11. 다시 시도해보세요.
12. 네, 좋습니다. 이번에는 전화가 울리네요.
13. 친구에게 얘기하세요.

90 Answering the Phone

A

1. It is Friday afternoon and your phone is ringing.
2. Pick up the receiver.
3. Answer the phone by saying "Hello."
4. It is your friend.
5. Let him/her speak.
6. He/she asks you if you have time for a movie.
7. Tell him/her you'd love to but you have an appointment.
8. Your friend feels sorry and you feel sorry, too.
9. Talk to your friend for a while.
10. Ask how he/she is doing.
11. He/she says everything's fine.
12. Tell him/her that you will call sometime later.
13. Say "Good bye." and hang up.

Key Vocabulary

- pick up: 전화를 받다
- receiver: 수화기
- have time for ~: ~를 위한 시간
- have an appointment: 약속이 있다.
- for a while: 한동안
- how he/she is dong: 그(녀)가 어떻게 지내는지
- call later: 나중에 전화 걸다
- hang up: 전화를 끊다.

B

1. It is Friday afternoon and your phone is __________.
2. Pick up the ___________.
3. Answer the phone by saying "Hello."
4. It is your friend.
5. ______ him/her speak.
6. He/she asks you if you have time ______ a movie.
7. Tell him/her you'd love to but you have an __________.
8. Your friend feels sorry and you feel sorry, too.
9. Talk to your friend ________ a while.
10. Ask ________ he/she is doing.
11. He/she says everything's fine.
12. Tell him/her that you will call sometime ________.
13. Say "Good bye." and ________ up.

C

1. 금요일 오후이고 당신의 전화가 울리네요.
2. 수화기를 집어 드세요.
3. "여보세요."라고 말하며 전화를 받으세요.
4. 친구네요.
5. 그(녀)가 말하도록 해주세요.
6. 그(녀)는 당신에게 영화 보러 갈 시간 있느냐고 물어봅니다.
7. 가고 싶지만 약속이 있다고 말하세요.
8. 친구가 유감스럽게 생각하고 당신 또한 그렇습니다.
9. 한동안 친구에게 얘기하세요.
10. 어떻게 지내냐고 물어보세요.
11. 그(녀)가 모든 일이 다 좋다고 말합니다.
12. 그(녀)에게 다음에 전화하겠다고 말하세요.
13. "안녕."이라고 말하고 전화를 끊으세요.

91 An Answering Machine

A

1. You need to go out and nobody is at home.
2. Turn on your answering machine.
3. Record an outgoing message on the machine.
4. When anyone calls you, he/she will hear the message.
5. Go out and return home in the evening.
6. You see the light blinking on the machine.
7. It means you have a message.
8. Press the button to play the message.
9. One of your friends called you and wants you to return his/her call.
10. Erase the message and turn off the machine.
11. Call your friend.

Key Vocabulary

- go out: 외출하다
- turn on: 켜다, 틀다
- answering machine: 응답기
- outgoing message: 외출한다는 메시지
- blinking: (불이) 깜박이는
- play the message: 메시지를 틀다
- return the call: 답신 전화를 걸다
- erase: 지우다
- turn off: 끄다

B

1. You need to go ______ and nobody is at home.
2. Turn _____ your answering machine.
3. Record an __________ message on the machine.
4. When anyone calls you, he/she will _______ the message.
5. Go out and ________ home in the evening.

6. You see the light _________ on the machine.
7. It means you have a __________.
8. Press the button to _______ the message.
9. One of your friends called you and wants you to _____ his/her call.
10. ________ the message and turn ______ the machine.
11. Call your friend.

C

1. 당신은 외출을 해야 하고 아무도 집에 없습니다.
2. 응답기를 켜세요.
3. 응답기에 외출 메시지를 녹음하세요.
4. 누군가 당신에게 전화를 걸면 그 메시지를 듣게 될 것입니다.
5. 외출을 하고 저녁에 돌아오세요.
6. 당신은 응답기에 불이 깜박이는 것을 봅니다.
7. 그것은 당신이 메시지를 받았다는 것을 의미합니다.
8. 버튼을 눌러서 메시지를 들어보세요.
9. 친구가 전화를 걸었고 당신이 전화를 걸어주길 원합니다.
10. 메시지를 지우고 응답기를 끄세요.
11. 친구에게 전화를 하세요.

92 Wrapping a Present

A

1. You're going to wrap a present for a friend.
2. Wrap the present in some tissue paper.
3. Put it in a box.
4. Put the box on some wrapping paper.
5. Wrap it up.
6. Fold the ends.
7. Take two pieces of tape.
8. Tape the ends of the package.
9. Cut a piece of ribbon.
10. Wrap it around the package.
11. Tie it in a knot.
12. Tie it in a bow.
13. Give it to your friend.

Key Vocabulary

- wrap: 싸다, 포장하다
- tissue paper: 박엽지, 투명한 얇은 종이
- wrapping paper: 포장지
- wrap up: 포장하다
- fold: 접다
- tape: 테이프, 테이프를 붙이다
- wrap A around B: A를 B 둘레에 두르다
- tie in a knot: 매듭을 묶다
- tie in a bow: 나비 모양으로 묶다

B

1. You're going to ________ a present for a friend.
2. Wrap the present in some __________ paper.
3. _______ it in a box.
4. Put the box on some ___________ paper.
5. Wrap it _______.
6. ________ the ends.
7. Take two __________ of tape.
8. ________ the ends of the package.
9. ______ a piece of ribbon.
10. Wrap it ___________ the package.
11. Tie it in a _______.
12. Tie it in a _______.
13. Give it to your friend.

C

1. 당신은 친구를 위해 선물을 포장하려 합니다.
2. 박엽지(투명한 얇은 종이)에 선물을 싸세요.
3. 그것을 박스에 넣으세요.
4. 박스를 포장지 위에다 놓으세요.
5. 포장하세요.
6. 끝을 접으세요.
7. 테이프 두 조각을 떼세요.
8. 꾸러미 양 끝에 테이프를 붙이세요.
9. 리본을 한 조각 자르세요.
10. 그것을 꾸러미 주위에 두르세요.
11. 매듭을 묶으세요.
12. 나비 모양으로 묶으세요.
13. 친구에게 선물을 주세요.

93 Opening a Present

A

1. Today is your birthday.
2. You got a package from the delivery person.
3. It is a birthday present from your friend.
4. The package is colorful and looks nice.
5. Look it over, feel it, and guess what's inside.
6. You cannot wait to see it.
7. Tear off the paper, wad it up and throw it away.
8. Now, carefully open the box.
9. Wow! It's exactly what you wanted!
10. Take it out carefully.
11. Put it on your desk and enjoy it.
12. Call your friend and say,
    "Thank you so much! I love it!"

Key Vocabulary

- package: 꾸러미, 소포
- delivery person: 배달원
- look over: 요리조리 살펴보다
- guess: 추측하다
- cannot wait to ~: ~하기위해 기다릴 수 없다
- tear off: 뜯다
- wad up: 구기다
- throw away: 버리다
- exactly: 정확하게, 바로
- take out: 꺼내다
- put A on B: A를 B위에 올리다
- so much = very much: 대단히
- I love it!: 아주 좋아!

B

1. Today is your birthday.
2. You got a package from the ________ person.
3. It is a birthday present ______ your friend.
4. The ________ is colorful and looks nice.
5. Look it _______, feel it, and ________ what's inside.
6. You cannot wait _____ see it.
7. Tear ______ the paper, wad it ____ and throw it ____.
8. Now, __________ open the box.
9. Wow! It's _________ what you wanted!
10. Take it _______ carefully.
11. _______ it on your desk and enjoy it.
12. Call your friend and say,
    "Thank you so much! I _______ it!"

C

1. 오늘은 당신의 생일입니다.
2. 배달원으로부터 소포를 하나 받았어요.
3. 친구에게서 온 생일선물이네요.
4. 소포가 화려하고 근사해보입니다.
5. 요리조리 살펴보고, 느껴보고, 무엇이 들었는지 추측해 보세요.
6. 보고 싶어서 기다릴 수가 없네요.
7. 종이를 뜯고, 구겨서 버리세요.
8. 자, 조심스럽게 박스를 여세요.
9. 와! 당신이 원했던 바로 그것이네요!
10. 조심스레 꺼내세요.
11. 책상 위에 놓고 즐기세요.
12. 친구에게 전화를 걸어 "정말 고마워! 너무 좋아!"라고 하세요.

94 Mailing a Document

A

1. You want to send some documents abroad.
2. Put the documents in a big envelop.
3. Write the address and seal it.

4. Take the envelop to the post office.
5. Pick up the waiting number from the machine.
6. Go sit on the sofa and wait for a while.
7. Your number is lighted and it's your turn.
8. Go to the window and say, "Registered, please."
9. The clerk asks you what's inside.
10. Tell him/her they are documents.
11. The clerk weighs the envelop and charges you.

12. Pay for the mail, get the receipt and leave the post office.

Key Vocabulary

- document: 서류
- address: 주소
- take A to B: A를 B로 가지고 가다
- pick up: 집다. 집어 들다
- for a while: 한동안
- window: 창구
- clerk: 직원, 서기
- weigh: 무게를 달다
- pay for ~: ~에 대해 값을 지불하다
- abroad: 외국으로, 외국에
- seal: 봉하다
- post office: 우체국
- waiting number: 대기번호
- be lighted: 불이 켜지다
- turn: 차례, 순서
- registered (mail): 등기 (우편)
- inside: 안에
- charge: 요금을 청구하다
- receipt: 영수증
- leave: 떠나다

B

1. You want to send some documents __________.
2. Put the documents in a big ____________.
3. Write the address and ___________ it.

4. ________ the envelop to the post office.
5. Pick up the waiting number _______ the machine.
6. Go sit on the sofa and wait _____ a while.
7. Your number is _________ and it's your ______.
8. Go to the _________ and say, "Registered, please."
9. The clerk asks you what's _________.

10. Tell him/her they are ___________.
11. The clerk ________ the envelop and charges you.
12. Pay ______ the mail, get the _______ and ________ the post office.

C

1. 당신은 서류를 외국으로 보내고 싶습니다.
2. 큰 봉투에 서류를 넣으세요.
3. 주소를 쓰고 봉하세요.
4. 봉투를 우체국으로 가져가세요.
5. 기계에서 대기번호를 뽑으세요.
6. 가서 소파에 앉아서 한동안 기다리세요.
7. 당신의 번호에 불이 켜졌습니다. 당신 차례입니다.
8. 창구로 가서 "등기로 해주세요."라고 말하세요.
9. 안에 무엇이 들었느냐고 직원이 묻습니다.
10. 서류라고 말하세요.
11. 직원이 봉투의 무게를 달고 당신에게 요금을 청구합니다.
12. 우편 요금을 내고, 영수증을 받고, 우체국을 떠나세요.

95 Mailing a Letter

A

1. You're going to write a letter to a friend.
2. Get an envelope and some paper.
3. Write the letter.
4. Sign your name at the bottom.
5. Fold up the letter.
6. Put it in the envelope.
7. Write your own name and address in the upper left-hand corner.
8. Write your friend's name and address in the middle of the envelope.
9. Tear off a stamp, lick it and stick it in the upper right-hand corner.
10. Take the letter to a mailbox near your house.
11. Drop it in the mailbox.
12. The mailman will pick it up by tomorrow.

Key Vocabulary

- stationery: 편지지
- in the middle of ~: ~중간에
- tear off: 뜯어내다
- stick: 붙이다
- upper left-hand corner: 왼쪽 위 코너
- lick: 침을 묻히다
- take A to B: A를 B로 가져가다
- drop A in B: A를 B안에 떨어뜨리다, 넣다
- pick up: 가져가다
- by tomorrow: 내일까지는

B

1. You're going to write a letter to a friend.
2. Get an ____________ and some stationery.
3. Write the letter.
4. Sign your name at the __________.
5. ________ up the letter.
6. Put it in the ____________.

7. Write your own name and address in the ________ left-hand corner.
8. Write your friend's name and address in the _________ of the envelope.
9. Tear ______ a stamp, lick it and _______ it in the upper right-hand corner.
10. Take the letter to a _______ near your house.
11. ________ it in the mailbox.
12. The mailman will _______ it up by tomorrow.

C

1. 당신은 친구에게 편지를 쓰려고 합니다.
2. 편지봉투 한 장과 편지지 몇 장을 가져오세요.
3. 편지를 쓰세요.
4. 끝에 사인을 하세요.
5. 편지를 접으세요.
6. 봉투에 그것을 넣으세요.
7. 당신 자신의 이름과 주소를 봉투 왼쪽 위에 적으세요.
8. 친구의 이름과 주소를 봉투 중간에 적으세요.
9. 우표를 한 장 떼어, 침을 발라 봉투 오른쪽 위에 붙이세요.
10. 집 근처 우체통으로 편지를 가져가세요.
11. 우체통에 넣으세요.
12. 우체부가 내일까지는 가져갈 겁니다.

96 A New Neighbor

A

1. You just moved into a new house.
2. You want to throw a party for your neighbors.
3. Check the calendar for the proper day.
4. Write and send the invitation cards.
5. Today is the big day.
6. Clean the house and decorate it with flowers.
7. Prepare delicious foods and set the table.
8. The guests arrive in time.
9. Greet them with a big smile and say "Welcome!"
10. The guests appreciate your invitation.
11. Ask them to have a seat and feel comfortable.
12. Serve them with the foods you prepared.
13. The guests enjoy talking over the foods.

Key Vocabulary

- move into ~: ~로 이사 들어오다
- throw a party: 파티를 열다
- proper: 적절한
- big day: 중대한 일이 있는 날
- decorate A with B: A를 B로 장식하다
- prepare: 준비하다
- set the table: 식탁을 차리다
- in time: 시간 안에
- greet A with B: A를 B로 맞이하다
- appreciate: 감사히 여기다, 감사하다
- ask A to B: A에게 B하기를 요청하다, 부탁하다
- feel comfortable: 편히 생각하다, 느끼다
- talk over the foods: 음식을 먹으면서 얘기하다

B

1. You just __________ into a new house.
2. You want to _________ a party for your neighbors.
3. Check the calendar _______ the proper day.

4. Write and send the ___________ cards.
5. Today is the _____ day.
6. Clean the house and __________ it with flowers.

7. ________ delicious foods and _____ the table.
8. The guests arrive ____ time.
9. _________ them with a big smile and say "Welcome!"
10. The guests ___________ your invitation.
11. Ask them to have a seat and feel _____________.
12. _________ them with the foods you prepared.
13. The guests enjoy talking ________ the foods.

C

1. 당신은 막 새집으로 이사를 왔습니다.
2. 당신은 이웃을 위해 파티를 열고 싶습니다.
3. 적절한 날이 언제인지 달력을 체크하세요.
4. 초대장을 써서 보내세요.
5. 오늘이 바로 그날입니다.
6. 집을 청소하고 꽃으로 장식하세요.
7. 맛있는 음식을 준비하고 식탁을 차리세요.
8. 손님들이 시간 안에 도착합니다.
9. 함박웃음으로 손님들을 맞이하고 “어서 오세요!”라고 말하세요.
10. 손님들이 초대를 감사하게 생각합니다.
11. 손님들에게 앉으시고 편히 생각하시라고 부탁하세요.
12. 당신이 준비한 음식으로 그들을 대접하세요.
13. 손님들은 음식을 먹으면서 대화를 즐깁니다.

97 Going to a Party

A

1. You are invited to your friend's birthday party.
2. The invitation card says it's 7 o'clock tonight.
3. Prepare a present and a card for your friend.
4. Wrap the present and sign the birthday card.

5. You arrive at your friend's in time.
6. At the party give your friend the present and the card.
7. The candles on the birthday cake are lighted.
8. Everyone sings "Happy Birthday."
9. Your friend blows out the candles.

10. He/She opens the presents and thanks for them.
11. He/She then serves a piece of the cake to everyone.
12. Everyone enjoys the cake.

Key Vocabulary

- be invited to ~: ~에 초대받다
- invitation card: 초대장
- prepare A for B: B를 위해 A를 준비하다
- wrap: 포장하다
- arrive at ~: ~에 도착하다
- your friend's = your friend's house: 친구 집
- candles are lighted: 촛불이 켜지다.
- blow out: 불어서 끄다
- thank for ~: ~에 대해 감사하다
- serve A to B: A를 B에게 대접하다
- a piece of ~: ~ 한 조각

B

1. You are __________ to your friend's birthday party.
2. The _________ card says it's 7 o'clock tonight.
3. ______________ a present and a card for your friend.
4. ________ the present and _______ the birthday card.
5. You arrive at your friend's in ________.

6. At the party give your friend the present and the card.
7. The candles on the birthday cake are __________.
8. Everyone sings "Happy Birthday."

9. Your friend ________ out the candles.
10. He/She ________ the presents and thanks for them.
11. He/She then ________ a piece of the cake to everyone.
12. Everyone ________ the cake.

C

1. 당신은 친구의 생일 파티에 초대받았습니다.
2. 초대장에는 오늘밤 7시라고 되어있습니다.
3. 친구를 위해서 카드와 선물을 준비하세요.
4. 선물을 포장하고 카드에 사인을 하세요.
5. 당신은 친구의 집에 도착합니다.
6. 파티에서 친구에게 선물과 카드를 주세요.
7. 생일 케이크 위의 초들에 불이 켜졌습니다.
8. 모두 "생일축하" 노래를 부릅니다.
9. 당신의 친구가 촛불을 불어서 끕니다.
10. 친구가 선물들을 열어보고 감사를 표합니다.
11. 그리고 친구는 케이크 한 조각씩을 모두에게 대접합니다.
12. 모두가 케이크를 즐깁니다.

98 A Fight

A

1. You are mad at your friend.
2. You want to fight with him.
3. Grab his/her bag away from him.
4. He shouts: "Hey! Give it back to me!"
5. Hold on to it. Don't let go.
6. Stick out your tongue at him.
7. Grab his arm and pull him.
8. Yell at him and punch him in the stomach.
9. Pinch his arm and squeeze his neck.
10. Kick him in the shins.
11. Hit him in the jaw and knock him out.

Key Vocabulary

- mad at ~: ~에 몹시 화가 난
- fight with ~: ~와 싸우다
- grab A away from B: A를 B에게서 잡아채다
- Hold on to it.: 꽉 붙들고 놓지 않다.
- stick out the tongue at ~: ~에게 혀를 내밀다
- grab: 붙들다
- pull: 당기다
- yell at ~: ~에게 소리치다
- punch A in B: A의 B를 치다
- pinch: 꼬집다
- squeeze: 비틀다
- kick A in B: A의 B를 발로 차다
- shin: 정강이
- jaw: 턱
- hit A in B: A의 B를 때리다
- knock out: 넘어뜨리다

B

1. You are ________ at your friend.
2. You want to ________ with him.
3. Grab his bag _________ from him.
4. He shouts: "Hey! Give it ________ to me!"
5. Hold _______ to it. Don't let _______.
6. Stick _______ your tongue at him.
7. Grab his arm, pull and _________ him.
8. Yell _____ him and ________ him in the stomach.
9. _________ his arm and __________ his neck.
10. __________ him in the shins.
11. Hit him in the jaw and knock him _____.

C

1. 당신은 친구에게 화가 났어요.
2. 당신은 그와 한판 싸우고 싶어요.
3. 그의 가방을 뺏어요.
4. 그가 소리치네요. "야, 그것 돌려줘!"
5. 꽉 쥐어요. 놓아주지 마세요.
6. 그에게 혀를 내미세요.
7. 그의 팔을 붙잡고 당겼다 미세요.
8. 그에게 소리를 지르고 배를 한 방 치세요.
9. 팔을 꼬집고 목을 비트세요.
10. 그의 정강이를 차세요.
11. 턱을 치고 넘어뜨리세요.

99 A Feast at Home

A

1. It's New Year's Eve.
2. You want to celebrate it with a feast.

3. Prepare delicious foods and drinks.
4. Set the table and light the candles.
5. Put all the foods and drinks on the table.
6. Call the family and invited guests to the table; "Time to eat!"

7. Everybody sits down at the table.
8. Serve the foods to each person.
9. Pass the rest of the foods around the table.
10. Everybody enjoys the foods and drinks.
11. Now, everybody is full and hilarious.
12. What a wonderful New Year's Eve!

Key Vocabulary

- New Year's Eve: 섣달 그믐날, 새해 전날
- celebrate A with B: A를 B로 기념하다
- prepare: 준비하다
- delicious: 맛있는
- set the table: 식탁을 차리다
- light the candle: 촛불을 켜다
- call A to B: A를 B로 부르다
- pass A around B: A를 B둘레로 돌리다
- full: 배부른, 가득 찬
- hilarious: 유쾌한, 즐거운
- What a wonderful ~! : 근사한 ~이다!

B

1. It's New Year's Eve.
2. You want to ____________ it with a feast.
3. Prepare ____________ foods and drinks.

4. _________ the table and ________ the candles.
5. Put all the foods and drinks on the table.
6. Call the people _____ the table; "Time to eat!"
7. Everybody sits down at the table.

8. ___________ the foods to each person.
9. ________ the rest of the foods around the table.
10. Everybody enjoys the foods and drinks.
11. Now, everybody is ________ and hilarious.
12. ________ a wonderful New Year's Eve!

C

1. 새해 전날입니다.
2. 당신은 그날을 연회로 기념하고 싶습니다.
3. 맛있는 음식과 마실 것들을 준비하세요.
4. 식탁을 차리고 촛불을 켜세요.
5. 음식과 마실 것들을 모두 식탁 위에 놓으세요.
6. 식구와 손님들을 식탁으로 부르세요. "식사 시간입니다!"
7. 모두가 식탁에 앉습니다.
8. 각자에게 음식들을 제공하세요.
9. 나머지 음식들은 테이블을 돌아가며 넘기세요.
10. 모든 사람들이 음식과 음료를 즐깁니다.
11. 이제, 모두 배가 부르고 즐겁습니다.
12. 근사한 새해 전날이네요!

100 Neighborhood Watch

A

1. You are on your way back home from work.
2. You witness a thief robbing your neighbor.
3. He holds a gun and a big bag.
4. You take out your cell phone and call the police.
5. The thief looks at you and runs away.
6. You chase after him and shout "Thief!"
7. Here comes a policeman!
8. The thief keeps on running.
9. He drops his gun and the bag too.
10. The policeman shouts "Stop!" and shoots at the sky.
11. The thief stops and holds up his hands.
12. The policeman puts handcuffs on the thief.
13. The thief regrets. But it's too late!

Key Vocabulary

- on your way back home: 집으로 돌아오는 길에
- witness: 목격하다
- take out: 꺼내다
- chase after: 뒤쫓아가다
- drop: 떨어뜨리다
- neighbor house: 이웃집
- run away: 도망치다
- keep on running: 계속해서 달리다
- shoot at ~: ~를 향해 총을 쏘다
- hold up hands: 양손을 위로 들다
- put handcuffs on ~: ~에 수갑을 채우다
- regret: 후회하다

B

1. You are on your ______ back home from work.
2. You ________ a thief robbing your neighbor.
3. He ________ a gun and a big bag.
4. You take ______ your mobile phone and call the police.
5. The thief looks at you and runs ________.
6. You ________ after him and shout "Thief!"
7. Here _______ a policeman!
8. The thief ________ on running.
9. He ________ his gun and the bag too.
10. The policeman shouts "Stop!" and ________ at the sky.
11. The thief stops and holds _____ his hands.
12. The policeman puts _________ on the thief.
13. The thief ________. But it's too _______!

C

1. 당신은 직장에서 집으로 돌아오는 길입니다.
2. 도둑이 한 이웃집을 터는 것을 목격합니다.
3. 그는 총과 큰 부대를 갖고 있습니다.
4. 당신은 휴대폰을 꺼내 경찰에 전화합니다.
5. 도둑은 당신을 보고 달아납니다.
6. 당신은 도둑을 뒤쫓아 가면서 "도둑이야!"라고 소리칩니다.
7. 경찰이 옵니다.
8. 도둑은 계속 달립니다.
9. 그는 총과 부대를 떨어뜨립니다.
10. 경찰이 "멈춰!"라고 소리치며 하늘을 향해 총을 쏩니다.
11. 도둑이 멈추며 두 손을 듭니다.
12. 경찰이 도둑에게 수갑을 채웁니다.
13. 도둑은 후회합니다. 하지만 너무 늦었습니다!

APPENDICES

APPENDIX A

Major Positions/Departments (주요 직책/부서)

Major Positions (주요 직책)	
회장	Chairman (of the Board)/Chairman of the Boarder of Directors/ Board Chairman
부회장	Vice Chairman (of the Board of Directors)
사장	President
사장보좌역	Assistant to President
부사장	Vice President/Executive Vice President
대표이사	Representative Director/Managing Director
전무이사	Executive Director/Senior Managing Director
상무이사	Managing Director/Executive Managing Director
이사	Director
중역(이사회)	Board of Directors
감사	Auditor
상담역(선임,원로)	Senior(Corporate) Advisor
고문	Advisor
부장, 본부장	General manager/Director
부장보좌역	Assistant to General Manager
영업부장	Manager Sales Division
인사부장	Manager Personnel Division
부국장	Deputy Director
실장	General Manager
국장보좌역	Assistant to Director
과장	Manager/Section Chief
영업과장	Section Chief Sales Division

Major Positions (주요 직책)	
인사과장	Section Chief Personnel Division
과장대리	Deputy Manager/Deputy Section Chief
과장보좌역	Assistant Manager
지점장(실장)	General manager
비서	Secretary
비서실	Secretariat
총무부	General Affairs Division(Div.)
홍보실	Public Relations Department(Dept.)
인사부	Personnel Division Div.
능력개발부	Personnel Development Div.
인재활용부	Personnel Utilization Div.
문서부	Legal Div.
통신부	Communication Div.
기획사업부	Corporate Planning Div.
해외사업부	Overseas Planning Div.
관련사업부	Affiliated Enterprises Div.

Names of Departments/Divisions (기구/회사 부서명)	
정보시스템부	Information Systems Div.
노동부	Labor Relations Div.
경리부	General Accounting Div.
재무부	Finance Div.
자금부	Finance Processing Div.
내부회계감사실	Internal Auditing Dept.
감사부	Inspection Div.
신용부	Credit Div.
영업부	Sales Div.

Names of Departments/Divisions (기구/회사 부서명)	
국내영업부	Domestic Sales Div
해외영업부	Overseas Sales Div.
판매관리부	Sales Administration Div.
판매영업부	Sales Affairs Div.

Major Positions (주요 직책)	
시장개발기술부	Marketing & Technical Service Div.
기자재부	Machinery & Materials Div.
구매부	Purchasing Div.
계약관리부	Contracts Planning Div.
연구기획부	R & D Planning and Coordination Div.
플랜트 엔지니어링 사업부	Plant Engineering Div.
설계부	Designing Div.
기술부	Technical Development Div.
중앙연구본부	Central R & D Bureau
개발기획본부	Project Planning & Development Bureau
기초연구소	Fundamental Research Laboratories
제품기술연구소	Products R & D Laboratories
생산기술연구소	Process Technology R & D Laboratories

정부 부처 (Government Ministeries & Offices)	
대통령	President
국무총리	Prime Minister
장관	Minister
차관	Vice Minister
차관보	Assiatant Minister

정부 부처 (Government Ministeries & Offices)	
청와대	Chong Wa Dae (the Blue House), the Presidential Office
국무총리실	Prime Minister's Office
재정경제부	Ministry of Finance and Economy
교육과학기술부	Ministry of Education, Science and Technology
외교통상부	Ministry of Foreign Affairs and Trade
행정자치부	Ministry of Administrations and Home Affairs
법무부	Ministry of Justice
국방부	Ministry of National Defence
통일부	Ministry of Unification
문화관광부	Ministry of Culture and Tourism
농림부	Ministry of Agriculture and Forestry
산업자원부	Ministry of Commerce, Industry and Energy
정보통신부	Ministry of Information and Communication
환경부	Ministry of Environment
보건복지부	Ministry of Health and Welfare
노동부	Ministry of Labor Affairs
여성가족부	Ministry of Gender Equality and Family
건설교통부	Ministry of Construction and Transportation
국토해양부	Ministry of Land, Transport and Maritime Affairs
기획예산처	Ministry of Planning and Budget
예산정책국	Budget & Policy Bureau
대통령비서실	Office of the President
경호실	Presidential Security Services
국무총리비서실	Prime Minister's Secretriat
국무회의	State Council
국민경제자문회의	National Economic Advisory Council
민주평화통일자문회의	Advisory Council on Democratic and Peaceful Unification

정부 부처 (Government Ministeries & Offices)	
국가과학기술자문회의	Presidential Advisory Council for Science & Technology
국가안정보장회의	National Security Council
건설교통위원회	Construction and Transportation Committee
감사원	Board of Audit and Inspection
국가정보원	National Intelligence Service
중앙인사위원회	Civil Service Commission
여성특별위원회	Presidential Commission on Womens Affairs
중소기업특별위원회	Presidential Commission on Small and Medium Business
법제처	Government Legislation Agency
법제실	Legislative Counseling Office
국가보훈처	Patriots and Veterans Administration Agency
공정거래위원회	Fair Trade Commission
금융감독위원회	Financial Supervisory Commission
금융감독원	Financial Supervisory Commission
청소년보호위원회	Commission of Youth Protection
국민고충처리위원회	Ombudsman of Korea
국무조정실	Office of Government Policy Coordination
비상기획위원회	Emergency Planning Commission
감사원	Board of Audit and Inspection
국세청	National Tax Service
관세청	Customs Service
조달청	Supply Administration
통계청	National Statistical Office
식품의약안전청	Korea Food & Drug Administration
해양경찰청	National Maritime Police Agency
검찰청	Public Prosecutors' Office

정부 부처 (Government Ministeries & Offices)	
경찰청	National Police Agency
서울지방경찰청	Seoul Metropolitan Police Agency
병무청	Military Manpower Administration
한국소비자보호원	Korea Consumer Protection Board
한국은행	Bank of Korea
대법원	Supreme Court
고등법원	High Court
법원	Court

국가상임위원회 및 특별위원회 (Standing Committee & Special Committee)	
국회운영위원회	House Steering Committee
법제사법위원회	Legislation and Judiciary committee
정무위원회	National Policy Committee
통일외교통상위원회	Unification, Foreign Affairs, and Trade Committee
국방위원회	National defence Committee
행정자치위원회	Government Administration and Local Autonomy Committee
교육위원회	Education Committee
과학기술정보통신위원회	Science, Technology, Information, & Telecommunication Committee
문화관광위원회	Culture and Tourism Committee
농림해양수산위원회	Agriculture, Forestry, Maritime Affairs, and Fisheries Committee
산업자원위원회	Commerce, Industry, and Energy Committee
보건복지위원회	Health and Welfare Committee
환경노동위원회	Environment and Labor Committee
건설노동위원회	Construction and Transportation Committee

국가상임위원회 및 특별위원회 (Standing Committee & Special Committee)	
정보위원회	Intelligence Committee
예산결산특별위원회	Special Committee on Budget and Accounts
윤리특별위원회	Special Committee on Ethics
여성특별위원회	Special Committee on Womens Affairs
실업대책특별위원회	Special Committee on Economic Reform and Unemployment
재해특별위원회	Special Committee on Disaster Prevention and Relief

정부 투자 기관 (Government Invested Company)	
농수산물유통공사	Agricultural and Fishery Marketing Cooperation
대한무역투자진흥공사	Korea Trade-Investment Promotion Agency
대한광업진흥공사	Korea resources Corporation
대한주택공사	Korea National Housing Corporation
한국토지공사	Korea Land Corporation
한국가스공사	Korea Gas Corporation
한국수자원공사	Korea Water Resources Corporation
한국담배인삼공사	Korea Tabacco & Ginseung Corporation
한국전력공사	Korea Electric Power Corporation
한국전기통신공사	Korea Telecom
농업협동조합중앙회	National Agricultural Cooperative Federation

APPENDIX B

Medical Departments in the Hospital (병원의 진료 부서)

내과	Internal Medicine
외과	General Surgery
흉부외과	Thoracic & Cardiovascular Surgery
신경외과	Neurosurgery
정형외과	Orthopedic Surgery
성형외과	Plastic & Reconstructive Surgery
산부인과	Obstetrics & Gynecology
피부과	Dermatology
비뇨기과	Urology
안과	Ophthalmology
이비인후과	Otorhinolaryngology
신경과	Neurology
마취통증학과	Anesthesiology pain medicine
가정의학과	Family Medicine
응급의학과	Emergency Medicine
재활의학과	Rehabilitation medicine
영상의학과	Radiology
방사선종양과	Radiation Oncology
핵의학과	Nuclear Medicine
진단검사의학과	Laboratory Medicine
병리과	Pathology
의공학과	Biomedical Engineering
장기이식센터	Organ Transplantation Service

APPENDIX C

Types of Jobs (직업의 종류)

accountant	회계사	dietitian	영양사
acupuncturist	침술사	director	감독
administrator	관리자	doctor	의사
agent	중개인	ecologist	생태학자
assistant	협력자, 조수	economist	경제학자
advisor	고문, 상담자	editor	편집인
analyst	분석가	electrician	전기기술자
archeologist	고고학자	employee	피고용인
architect	건축가	employer	고용인
artist	예술가	engineer	공학자, 기술자
attorney	변호사	executive	이사, 간부
author	작가	fashion designer	패션 디자이너
baker	빵 제조업자	fire fighter	소방수
banker	은행가	florist	꽃장수
barber	이발사	flight attendant	비행기 승무원
broker	중개상	foreman	작업감독
butcher	푸줏간주인	fund raiser	자금조달자
cameraman	촬영기사	fund manager	자금관리자
carpenter	목수	gardner	정원사
chiropractor	척추지압사	geneticist	유전학자
computer programmer	컴퓨터 프로그래머	geologist	지질학자
consultant	고문, 상담자	graphic designer	그래픽 디자이너
coordinator	제작진행책임자	greengrocer	청과물상인
copywriter	광고문안가	guide	안내인
counsellor	상담자	hair dresser	미용사
critic	비평가	horticulturalist	원예가
deliveryman	배달인	housekeeper	주부
dentist	치과의사	inspector	검사관
designer	디자이너	instructor	교관, 지도자

interpreter	통역관	producer	프로듀서, 저작자
janitor	청소부, 관리인	professor	교수
jeweler	보석상인	promoter	흥행기획자
journalist	신문잡지업자	psychologist	심리학자
locksmith	자물쇠장수	psych therapist	심리치료사
manager	경영자, 지배인	real estate agent	부동산 업자
mechanic	기계공, 수리공	receptionist	접수원
merchant	상인	repair person	수리공
messenger	심부름꾼, 배달인	reporter	통신원
meteorologist	기상학자	sales person	판매원
microbiologist	미생물학자	sales clerk	판매서기
midwife	산파, 조산원	scientist	과학자
musician	음악가	secretary	비서
nutritionist	영양학자	security guard	안전요원
newscaster	뉴스진행자	shop worker	가게점원
nurse	간호사	social worker	사회사업가
operator	전화교환수, 조작자	solicitor	법무관
ophthalmologist	안과학자	sports person	스포츠인
optician	안경장수	statistician	통계학자
painter	페인트공	stock broker	주식중개인
paramedic	준의료종사자	stylist	디자이너
pharmacist	약사	supervisor	감독
photographer	사진사	surgeon	외과의사
teller	금전출납계산원	surveyor	측량사
therapist	치료전문가	tailor	재봉사
traffic controller	교통통제관	travel agent	여행업자
translator	번역가	treasurer	회계원
podiatrist	족병치료사(학자)	weather forecaster	일기 예보관
police officer	경찰관	zoo keeper	동물원 관리인
politician	정치가	etc.	등등.

APPENDIX D

How Do You Feel Today? (오늘 기분 어때요?)

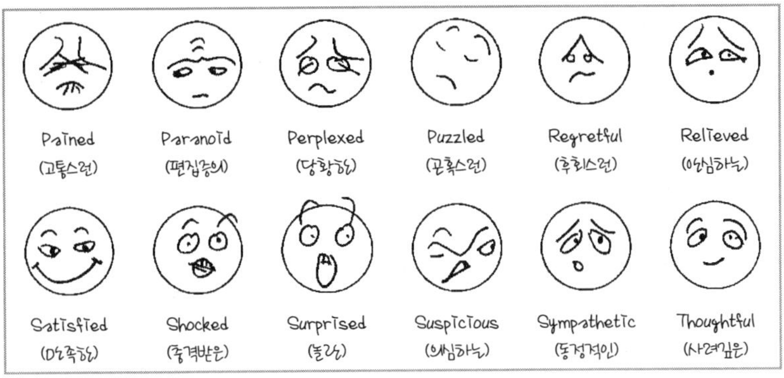
Pained
(고통스런)
Paranoid
(편집증의)
Perplexed
(당황한)
Puzzled
(곤혹스런)
Regretful
(후회스런)
Relieved
(안심하는)
Satisfied
(만족한)
Shocked
(충격받은)
Surprised
(놀란)
Suspicious
(의심하는)
Sympathetic
(동정적인)
Thoughtful
(사려깊은)

제2판

액션시리즈로 배우는

생활영어

지은이 김성애
펴낸이 조경희
펴낸곳 경문사
펴낸날 2011년 6월 1일 1판 1쇄
2018년 6월 1일 2판 1쇄
등 록 1979년 11월 9일 제313-1979-23호
주 소 04057, 서울특별시 마포구 와우산로 174
전 화 (02)332-2004 팩스 (02)336-5193
이메일 kyungmoon@kyungmoon.com
facebook facebook.com/kyungmoonsa

값 12,000원

ISBN 979-11-6073-143-9

★ 경문사 홈페이지에 오시면 즐거운 일이 생깁니다.
http://www.kyungmoon.com